A Revelation of Purgatory by an Unknown, Fifteenth-Century Woman Visionary: Introduction, Critical Text, and Translation

Marta Powell Harley

Studies in Women and Religion
Volume 18

The Edwin Mellen Press
Lewiston/Queenston

Library of Congress Cataloging-in-Publication Data

Harley, Marta Powell.
   A revelation of purgatory by an unknown, fifteenth-century woman visionary.

   (Studies in women and religion ; v. 18)
   Bibliography: p.
   1. Revelation of purgatory. 1. Purgatory--Early works to 1800. 3. Visions--Early works to 1800. 4. Private revelations--Early works to 1800. I. Title. II. Series.
   BT840.R483H37   1985   236'.5   ISBN 0-88946-531-2

This is volume 18 in the continuing series
Studies in Women and Religion
Volume 13 ISBN 0-88946-531-2
SWR Series ISBN 0-88946-549-5

The Edwin Mellen Press   The Edwin Mellen Press
Box 450   Box 67
Lewiston, New York   Queenston, Ontario
USA   14092   CANADA   L0S 1L0

Printed in the United States of America

A Revelation of Purgatory by an Unknown, Fifteenth-Century Woman Visionary: Introduction, Critical Text, and Translation

For My Parents

ACKNOWLEDGMENTS

I wish to acknowledge that the section on date, origin, and authorship will appear in a forthcoming issue of <u>Reading Medieval Studies</u>.

For kindly making the Longleat, Bodleian, and Thornton manuscripts available to me, I am grateful to Jane Fowles, Librarian, Longleat House; David Vaisey, Keeper, Department of Western Manuscripts, The Bodleian Library; and Joan Williams, Librarian, Lincoln Cathedral Library. I was aided in the historical research by the courteous archivists and librarians in Winchester at the Hampshire Record Office and the Cathedral Library, and I received very helpful correspondence from Michael Benskin, A. I. Doyle, and Angus McIntosh.

I am especially grateful to Germaine Greer and the Tulsa Center for the Study of Women's Literature for a 1982 summer bursary for research in England, and to Professor Herbert Richardson and the Edwin Mellen Press for making this publication possible.

TABLE OF CONTENTS

INTRODUCTION

CRITICAL TEXT

TRANSLATION

WORKS CONSULTED

INTRODUCTION

Preface

The fifteenth-century prose work A Revelation of Purgatory is a holy woman's dream vision of a nun's progress through the pains of purgatory. The piece survives in three manuscripts: Longleat MS. 29 (L), fols. 155r-165v; the Thornton Manuscript (Lincoln Cathedral MS. 91) (T), fols. 250v-258r; and Bodleian MS. Eng. th. c. 58 (B), fols. 10r-12v. A critical edition of the text has never before been published. In 1895 Carl Horstman printed, without commentary, the incomplete Thornton Manuscript text (unaware of either L or B) in the appendix to Yorkshire Writers, therein entitled A Revelation respecting Purgatory.[1]

Horstman's transcription attracted only occasional notice. In 1910 Geraldine E. Hodgson mentioned A Revelation of Purgatory in her introduction to The Form of Perfect Living and Other Prose Treatises by Richard Rolle of Hampole, but just as she erred in ascribing the "other prose treatises" to Rolle, she wrongly ascribed A Revelation of Purgatory to him:

---

[1] 2 vols. (New York, 1895) 1:383-92. Although currently unavailable, Sarah Jane Ogilvie-Thomson's D. Phil. dissertation, "An Edition of the English Works in MS. Longleat 29 excluding 'The Parson's Tale,'" Oxford U, 1980, includes a transcription of L's version of A Revelation of Purgatory. The critical edition on which this published edition is based is Marta Powell Harley, "A Revelation of Purgatory: A Critical Edition Based on Longleat MS. 29," diss., Columbia U, 1981.

> There is among his [Rolle's] voluminous
> writings, a curious and interesting <u>Reve-
> lation concerning Purgatory</u>, purporting to be
> a dream about one, Margaret, a soul in
> Purgatory. Amidst much natural horror, not
> however exceeding that described by Dante,
> there are many quaint side-lights thrown upon
> our forefathers' ways of thought; as <u>e.g.</u>,
> when Margaret's soul is weighed in one scale,
> against the fiend, and a great long worm with
> him, in the other; the worm of conscience, in
> fact.[2]

Rotha Mary Clay, in <u>The Hermits and Anchorites of
England</u>, echoed one of Hodgson's adjectives in a 1914
reference to "the curious <u>Revelation respecting Purga-
tory</u>,"[3] and in 1927 Hope Emily Allen, in <u>Writings
Ascribed to Richard Rolle</u>, gave us another glimpse into
the "natural horror," when, commenting on the inclusion
of <u>A Revelation of Purgatory</u> in both Longleat MS. 29
and the Thornton Manuscript, she transcribed in a
footnote a passage from Longleat's description of the
sensational torments of sinful priests.[4] Morton
Bloomfield included <u>A Revelation of Purgatory</u> in his
1952 study <u>The Seven Deadly Sins</u>,[5] giving the piece its

------

[2](London: Baker, 1910) xvii-xviii.

[3](1914; Detroit: Singing Tree P, 1968) 154.

[4](London: Oxford UP, 1927) 36.

[5](n.p.: Michigan State College P, 1952) 221.

first direct attention, and that without over-emphasizing the visions's curiosity or sensationalism. However, notwithstanding his appraisal of the work as "an extremely vivid otherworld vision which deserves further study," the vision has received no scholarly attention.

The inclusion of <u>A Revelation of Purgatory</u> in two prominent fifteenth-century anthologies, Longleat 29 and the Thornton Manuscript,[6] speaks for its original appeal. That the few scholars who have noticed the piece have found it remarkable encourages the hope that this presentation of the work will gain a wider audience for this "extremely vivid" account of a medieval woman's vision of the Christian afterlife. The introduction offers background sections on the doctrine of purgatory, on the Christian afterlife in popular visions and the <u>Revelation</u>, and on the woman visionary.

---

[6]A facsimile of the Thornton Manuscript has been published: D. S. Brewer and A. E. B. Owen, introd., <u>The Thornton Manuscript (Lincoln Cathedral MS. 91)</u> (London: Scolar P, 1975). For a review of the volume and a reply to the review, see <u>The Times Literary Supplement</u>, 22 July 1977 and 19 August 1977.

The Doctrine of Purgatory

According to Church teaching, purgatory is "a place or condition of temporal punishment for those who, departing this life in God's grace, are not entirely free from venial faults, or have not fully paid the satisfaction due to their transgressions."[7]

Scriptural support for the doctrine of purgatory is slight.[8] In the Old Testament, 2 Machabees 12.39-46 supports the doctrine of purgatory. Judas Machabeus sends 12,000 silver drachmas to Jerusalem as a sin offering for the fallen soldiers who had, contrary to Jewish law, worn amulets in combat. The offering expresses belief both in ultimate resurrection and in the efficacy of prayer and atonement for the dead: "It is therefore a holy and wholesome thought to pray for the dead, that they may be loosed from sins" (2 Mac. 12.46). In the New Testament, Matthew 12.32 suggests a process of forgiveness in the afterlife: "And, whosoever shall speak a word against the Son of man, it shall be forgiven him; but he that shall speak against

---

[7] Edward J. Hanna, "Purgatory," The Catholic Encyclopedia, 1913 ed.

[8] The three scriptural passages that follow, all quoted from the Rheims-Douay translation of The Holy Bible, are referred to in Hanna and in J. F. X. Cevetello and R. J. Bastian, "Purgatory," The New Catholic Encyclopedia, 1967 ed. A. Michel discusses these and nine additional New Testament passages that "supposent l'existence du purgatoire," though they do not offer "un enseignement direct," in "Purgatoire," Dictionnaire de théologie catholique, 1936 ed.

the Holy Ghost, it shall not be forgiven him, neither
in this world, nor in the world to come." According to
1 Corinthians 3.11-15, the durability of each person's
work will be tested by fire after death: "If any man's
work abide, which he hath built thereupon, he shall
receive a reward. If any man's work burn, he shall
suffer loss; but he himself shall be saved, yet so as
by fire." This passage has served as "le texte
classique sur lequel beaucoup de théologiens se sont
fondés pour affirmer l'existence du purgatoire."[9]

Though the scriptural evidence is not
considerable, the "doctrine that many who have died are
still in a place of purification and that prayers avail
to help the dead is part of the very earliest Christian
tradition."[10] The writings of the Fathers and the
liturgy of the early Church make clear the teaching.[11]
The dogma of purgatory received "sa formulation
définitive aux trois conciles généraux de Lyon (1274),
de Florence (1439) et de Trente (1563)."[12] At the
Council of Lyon (of the three, the only Council earlier
than the Revelation), the Church declared its faith in
a place of purification and in the value of the suf-
frages of the living for the dead.

_____

[9]Michel, "Purgatoire."

[10]Hanna.

[11]See Cevetello and Bastian; Hanna; and Michel,
"Purgatoire."

[12]Michel, "Purgatoire."

The Church, however, made no solemn statements on
the quality or length of purgatorial punishment. The
nature of the punishment has been commonly conceived as
both negative--"the temporary deprivation of the
beatific vision"--and positive--a "pain of sense."
Among the Fathers and later theologians, the purgative
agent was generally assumed to be fire, an assumption
founded primarily on 1 Cor. 3.11-15, but the Councils
remained silent on the matter.[13] That the punishment
is finite is implicit in the very nature of purgatory;
the souls, once thoroughly purified, are received "mox
in caelum."[14]

---

[13]Cevetello and Bastian. The differences between
the Eastern Church and the West concerning both the
state of souls immediately after death and their
purification by fire thus went unresolved. A. Michel
discusses the latter disagreement in "Feu du
Purgatoire," Dictionnaire de théologie catholique, 1936
ed.

[14]From the text of the Council of Lyon, as quoted
by Michel, "Purgatoire."

The Christian Afterlife in Popular
Visions and the *Revelation*

In contrast to the Church's unelaborated
definition of purgatory, popular visions from the
earliest centuries of the Church through the fifteenth
century supplied detailed descriptions of the Christian
otherworld, its terrain, its inhabitants, and their
horrific misfortunes.[15] While the exaggerated
details--the snakes, the iron hooks in the heart, the
vats of boiling pitch--are certainly without Church
authority, the general conceptions of the afterlife
often do reflect the broad beliefs of the Church. A
Revelation of Purgatory, a latecomer to this literary

---

[15]For a systematic account of the earlier visions,
see Harold W. Attridge, "Greek and Latin Apocalypses,"
and Adela Yarbro Collins, "The Early Christian
Apocalypses," in Apocalypse: The Morphology of a
Genre, ed. John J. Collins, Semeia 14 (1979): 159-86,
61-122. Important for Apocryphal apocalypses is E.
Hennecke, New Testament Apocrypha, ed. W. Schnee-
melcher, trans. R. McL. Wilson, 2 vols. (London:
Lutterworth P, 1965) vol. 2. Three works supplying
summaries of medieval visions are John D. Seymour,
Irish Visions of the Other-World (New York: MacMillan,
1930); Howard R. Patch, The Other World According to
Descriptions in Medieval Literature, Smith College
Studies in Modern Languages ns 1 (Cambridge, Mass.:
Harvard UP, 1950); and D. D. R. Owen, The Vision of
Hell: Infernal Journeys in Medieval French Literature
(Edinburgh: Scottish Academic P, 1970). On medieval
English visions, see Arnold B. van Os, Religious
Visions (Amsterdam: Paris, 1932); and Frances A.
Foster, "Legends of the After-Life," in A Manual of the
Writings in Middle English: 1050-1500, gen. eds. J.
Burke Severs and Albert E. Hartung, 6 vols. to date
(Hamden, Conn.: Conn. Acad. of Arts and Sciences,
1967-) 2:452-57, 645-49.

genre,[16] respects the general doctrine while showing a
thoroughgoing familiarity with this body of
writings--beginning, in fact, with the dream's
occurrence on St. Lawrence's night, the date likewise
of Guillaume de Deguileville's <u>Pylgremage of the
Sowle</u>.[17] Thus, our discussion of the purgatory
depicted in the <u>Revelation</u> invites a double focus.
First, we may ask how well the <u>Revelation</u> reflects
Church teaching: Is purgatory a distinct state? Is
purgatorial punishment negative, positive, or both? Is
there a sense of progressive purgation? And are the
intercessions of the faithful efficacious in relieving
the suffering of the souls in purgatory? Second, as we
address these questions, we may ask to what extent <u>A</u>

----

[16]For a discussion of apocalyptic writings as a
literary genre, "a group of written texts marked by
distinctive recurring characteristics which constitute
a recognizable and coherent type of writing," see John
J. Collins, "Introduction: Towards the Morphology of a
Genre," in <u>Apocalypse: The Morphology of a Genre</u>, ed.
John J. Collins, <u>Semeia</u> 14 (1979): 1-20. The strong
literary character of the early Christian apocalypses
has been remarked: "Considering the traditional
character of the imagery and the manner of its
composition, the question arises how far the
apocalyptic visions are true to experience. . . . [T]he
work of distinguishing neatly between actual experience
and literary activity in the Apocalypses will scarcely
be successful" (Hennecke 584).

[17]Editions of this work include Guillaume de
Deguileville, <u>The Pylgremage of the Sowle</u>, The English
Experience: Its Record in Early Printed Books
Published in Facsimile 726 (Norwood, N. J.: Johnson,
1975); and Guillaume De Guileville, <u>The Booke of the
Pylgremage of the Sowle</u>, ed. Katherine Isabella Cust
(London, 1859).

Revelation of Purgatory reflects the conceptions of the
Christian afterlife found in the popular visions.

In A Revelation of Purgatory purgatory is clearly
a distinct state; the Christian afterlife is, in fact,
divided into the traditional four regions: hell,
purgatory, the earthly paradise, and heaven. Margaret,
the spirit in purgatory, can report no more of hell
than that the worm of conscience is its "grettest
peyne" (201), though she suggests that her inability is
due to a lack of permission (211-13). Likewise, there
is no description of heaven in the Revelation; the
vision closes with Margaret approaching the golden
gate. The slight attention given to hell and heaven is
in accord with Margaret's remark to the visionary, "I
tel the som party of helle and some partie of heuyn"
(219-20). Details of the earthly paradise are
sufficient to create a scene. In the earthly paradise,
which is separated from purgatory by the "stronge
brygge" (873), Margaret is washed in the well of grace
and married to Christ in a white chapel.

The Revelation's representation of purgatory
within a four-part division of the Christian afterlife
is not surprising. Among popular accounts, Bede's
Vision of Drythelm in the Historia ecclesiastica offers
the "earliest example" of the "belief in purgatory as a
distinct and separate state" and thus represents the
eschatological views of the Anglo-Saxon Church, which
"held continuously . . . that from Hell there could be
no deliverance at any time, but that there was a

Purgatory in the intermediate state."[18]   In contrast,
the Irish Church, prior to the approximate date 1000,
"drew no such hard-and-fast distinction between Hell
and Purgatory, but invested the former region with
purgatorial qualities, and admitted that from it souls
could be freed"; representing the post-1000 period in
which purgatory "emerges as a distinct state" are the
twelfth-century Vision of Tundale and Legend of Saint
Patrick's Purgatory,[19] visions which likewise evidence
a four-part Christian otherworld.

---

[18]Seymour 48, 57. For Drythelm's vision, see
Bede, Historia ecclesiastica, ed. Bertram Colgrave and
R. A. B. Mynors (Oxford: Oxford UP, 1969) 488-98.
This four-part division is anticipated in the
Apocalypse of Paul, wherein Paul sees two visions of
paradise (the Holy Jerusalem of the canonical
Apocalypse of John and the Edenic earthly paradise) and
a vision of hell that implies a distinction between
temporary and eternal punishment: the punishments in
the lake of fire appear purgatorial when compared to
the punishment in the abyss into which unbelievers are
cast. For H. Duensing's translation of the Apocalypse
of Paul, see Hennecke 755-98. On the inception of the
idea of purgatory, see R. W. Southern's review of
Jacques le Goff's La Naissance du Purgatoire (Paris,
1982) in The Times Literary Supplement 12 June 1982:
651-52. Le Goff dates "the birth of Purgatory" late in
the twelfth century, his reasoning being "that the word
Purgatory did not exist before this date": "Un lieu
innomme n'existe pas tout a fait." Recalling Drythelm
and Saint Patrick's Purgatory, Southern admits that he
is "not convinced that anything new came into existence
with the word." He observes that, "Ill-defined though
it was, the idea of Purgatory was deeply rooted in
theological tradition," and he dates the maturation of
the idea in the mid-eleventh century.

[19]Seymour 57, 16. The Vision of Tundale,
internally dated 1149, was originally written in Latin
(Footnote Continued)

Typical of those in the earlier afterlife visions, the purgatorial punishments in A Revelation of Purgatory are emphatically physical. The pain of loss is more often ignored in these works of "spiritual shock treatment."[20]   In A Revelation of Purgatory the punishment is primarily by fire, as souls move through three consecutive fires. For the seven deadly sins, souls are punished in the first fire. Seven devils administer torments that often well suit the sin: for example, the hook-lined gown and headdress of adders appropriately scourge Margaret's pride (248ff), while a meal of snakes and adders and a drink of "al maner cursed venym" (295-96) requite her gluttony.[21]

While I find no antecedents in the visionary literature for the dog and cat that harry Margaret throughout the first fire, the great majority of the physical punishments in A Revelation of Purgatory are common to earlier and contemporary afterlife visions.

(Footnote Continued)
and later translated into Italian, German, Dutch, and English; the Middle English couplet version, which survives in five fifteenth-century manuscripts, is in an early printing: The Visions of Tundale, ed. W. B. D. D. Turnbull (Edinburgh, 1843). The legendary visit of Owen to Saint Patrick's purgatorial cave in 1153 is recounted in Latin and French versions and survives as well in six Middle English verse accounts and two prose versions. For a Middle English prose version, see George Philip Krapp, The Legend of Saint Patrick's Purgatory (Baltimore: Murphy, 1900).

[20]D. D. R. Owen 7.

[21]The organization recalls the seven cornices of Dante's Mount Purgatory. On the Revelation's use of the sins, see Bloomfield 221.

Souls suffer in fiery pits (357), recalling the river
of fire in the Apocalypse of Paul, or revolve on fiery
wheels (449), as in the Apocalypse of Peter and Saint
Patrick's Purgatory (see explanatory note 449). The
transfer of Margaret from the "grete blake watyr . . .
þat semed as cold as eny yse" (301-02) into "a gret
fyr" (307) recalls similar contrasts in earlier
visions; for example, in Plutarch's Vision of
Thespesius, souls move from a lake of boiling gold into
a lake of chilling lead, while in Drythelm, souls are
cast from one side of a vale to the other, alternately
experiencing extreme heat and cold.[22] In the
Revelation, purgatorial souls endure the violent
hammering of demonic smiths, a punishment found in
Thespesius, the Voyage of Saint Brendan, and Tundale
(see explanatory note 382ff). The transformation of
Margaret's soul from black to red to white recalls the
Vision of Thespesius; as the souls pass through the
three lakes, they undergo a similar change in color:
". . . when the souls had grown red hot in the gold
from the blazing heat, the daemons plunged them into
the lake of lead; when they had there been chilled and
hardened, like hailstones, they were removed to the
lake of iron. Here they turned an intense black. . .
."[23] Even the worm of conscience, which Hodgson

_____

[22]Plutarch, "on the Delays of the Divine
Vengeance," in Moralia, trans. Phillip H. de Lacy and
Benedict Finarson, 15 vols. (Cambridge, Mass.: Harvard
UP, 1968) 7:170-299.

[23]Plutarch 295. In Dante's Purgatorio 9.94-105,
                                    (Footnote Continued)

mentions as a "quaint side-light thrown upon our forefathers' ways of thought," has a clear antecedent in the vision literature, appearing in Deguileville's Pylgremage of the Sowle (see explanatory note 199-200). Further, the violence in the Revelation is heightened in two conventional ways: the expectation and absence of a guide and the threat of the visionary's physical suffering (see explanatory notes 16 and 70-72).

In A Revelation of Purgatory the kinds (and numbers) of punishments found in such visions as Paul, Tundale, and the Legend of Saint Patrick's Purgatory are incorporated into a dual tripartite plan depicting a progressive transformation of the individual soul. Such dramatizations of progress through purgatory are not common to the earlier visions. For example, in Bede's Drythelm souls must endure alternating heat and cold until their release on the Day of Judgment. Likewise, in Tundale souls experience constant cyclical torment until Judgment: for example, souls melt on a grate, only to be reconstituted to melt again, while the beast on the frozen lake consumes and eliminates souls in an endless cycle.

The purgatorial spirit, Margaret, moves through three contiguous fires, the first two purging mortal and venial sins and the third completing the cleansing. Margaret expands the conception of purgatory by

---

(Footnote Continued)
the three steps leading to the gate of purgatory are white, black, and red, representing the three stages of penitence -- confession, contrition, and satisfaction. Dante, Purgatory, trans. Dorothy L. Sayers (1955; New York: Penguin, 1969) 136-37, 139.

introducing, in addition to the purgatory of
righteousness (i.e., the "general purgatory" of the
three fires), two more purgatories--the purgatory of
mercy and the purgatory of grace. Within this plan
there are inconsistencies, which bear some
consideration.

At 684, after Margaret has passed from the "grete
fyr" through the "medel fyr" and finally the "þrid
fyr," thereby undergoing a transformation from black to
red to white, she tells the dreamer, "þer bene thre
purgatories." However, although we expect a
correlation of the three purgatories with the three
fires, she continues, "þat one is þe grete fyr of
purgatory þat þou saw me in fyrst, and þat is euyn-lyke
to þe peynes of helle, save we shal be saved and þay
noȝt. And þese other two fyres bene accounted
an-other" (684-88). We are left in doubt about the
nature of the third purgatory, as a discussion of the
sufferers in the three fires follows. Subsequently,
Margaret summarizes, "I haue declared to þe þese bittyr
peynes of purgatory, and I wold declar þe two moo
purgatories, bot I may noȝt lange abide. Bot þis is þe
general purgatory for al men þat bene Cristen"
(760-64). This statement contradicts the previous
claim that the "grete fyr" is one purgatory and the
other two the second of three; here all three fires are
one purgatory ("general purgatory") and two more
purgatories are evidently to remain undefined.

Abruptly contradicting her claim that she has no
time to describe the two other purgatories, Margaret at
once describes the purgatory of mercy and the purgatory
of grace, but these two purgatories are ill-defined
and, in fact, detract from the conception of purgatory

developed in the three fires. The three fires provide
a reasonable graduation of purgatorial punishment for
"al men þat bene Cristen." The great fire punishes
those who fail to do penance for deadly sins confessed
in life and those who make confession at the point of
death (703ff). Those whose venial sins are only
generally shriven and those whose penance is
insufficient forego the great fire and enter the middle
fire (732ff). Without entering the first two fires,
those whose penance was fulfilled at death go only
through the third fire (745ff).

The purgatory of mercy (765-73) overlaps with the
conception of the third fire, the destination of, among
others, "innocentȝ . . . and al holy martires"
(749-51). The purgatory of mercy is for those who have
"by sekenesse and grete tribulacions in þis wor[l]de"
purchased more than adequate pardon--a criterion that
the "holy martires" of the third fire would surely have
met.

The description of the purgatory of grace (774ff)
is inadequate. Within this definition, as within the
broad representation of three purgatories, there is
apparent improvisation or afterthought: Margaret
defines the purgatory of grace as punishment on earth
at the point of the sin, but after summarily saying,
"And þat es called þe purgatorye of grace" (778-79),
she extends her definition of the purgatory of grace to
include the remission of punishment that those to whom
spirits appear earn on behalf of the suffering spirits.

Perhaps the impulse to divide purgatory into
three regions, or into two tripartite schemes, can be
attributed to the influence of other such revelations.
For example, among the Revelations of Saint Bridget

(1303-73) is a vision of "the dome of a sowle whome the
fend accused," in which purgatory is divided into three
areas: immediately beyond the darkness surrounding
hell's furnace is "the greteste payne of purgatorie,"
where there is "towchyng of fendes," "venemouse
wormes," "bestes," heat and cold, darkness and
confusion; those in the second place suffer exhaustion,
a "defaute of myghtes"; and the souls in the third
place suffer "no payne bot desyre of comyng to the
presence of God and to his blessed syght." Those who
lived "innocentely" or who "so amended her synnes with
good werkes" immediately enjoy the presence of God,
avoiding the three divisions of purgatory.[24] This
graduation of punishment (from physical torment, to
physical weakness, to the pain of separation from God),
along with the condition that some souls bypass
purgatory altogether, broadly parallels the
Revelation's tripartite division of "general purgatory"
into three graduated fires and its identification of
two additional purgatories to accommodate souls for
whom any punishment would seem unjust.

A similar division of purgatory is offered by the
visionary St. Frances of Rome (1384-1440).[25] In her
plan, two of three divisions are further divided into
three areas. Bordering hell is "le Purgatoire

---

[24]The Revelations of Saint Birgitta, ed. William
P. Cumming, EETS es 178 (London: Oxford UP, 1929) 43,
46-49.

[25]Butler's Lives of the Saints, ed., rev., and
suppl. Herbert Thurston and Donald Attwater, 4 vols.
(London: Burns and Oates, 1956) 1:529-33.

inférieur," a clear fire wherein priests and bishops
suffer more than men and women religious and clerks not
yet ordained as priests, who in turn suffer more than
lay men and women with unexpiated grave faults. Above
"le Purgatoire inférieur" is "la region moyenne, ou
elle [St. Frances] vit écrit en grosses lettres le mot:
Purgatoire." The region is subdivided into three
torments--a frozen lake and vats of boiling oil and
burning metal. The third region, that most remote from
hell, is the destination of those who must suffer only
light, short-term pains or the pain of loss.[26] The
Revelation's "general purgatory" comprehends St.
Frances's "Purgatoire" and "Purgatoire inférieur," for
in the Revelation particular attention is given to the
exceptional torments of sinful priests, religious men
and women, and especially sinful married or single men
and women. St. Frances's superior region corresponds
with the Revelation's third fire and its purgatories of
mercy and grace.

　　While the Revelation's ties to St. Bridget's and
St. Frances's conceptions of purgatory may not be
direct (indeed, St. Frances's dates would make
influence unlikely), the existence of these two
near-contemporary visions of purgatory shows the
traditional character of the Revelation's conceptions.
The chief contribution of these graduations of
purgatory is that they make possible a physical
dramatization of a soul's progressive purgation in the

---

[26]M. L'abbé Louvet, Le Purgatoire d'après les
révélations des saints, 3rd ed. (Paris, 1893) 90-91.

Christian afterlife. In no vision is this more
emphatically depicted than in the Revelation, where we
see the soul's change in the three fires of "general
purgatory."

As a final test of the soul, however, weighing is
common in the afterlife visions. For example, in
Turpin's vision of Charlemagne, "all the good works of
Charlemagne were laid in one scale, with the wood and
the stones of the churches, monasteries, etc. which he
had built. In the other scale demons put his crimes
and sins. His good deeds being heavier, the demons
were driven away. . . ."[27] In the Revelation the
visionary's pilgrimage on Margaret's behalf is the good
deed that brings Margaret "doun to þe fayr lady" and
causes the devil and the worm of conscience to be
"voidet away" (862-63). Margaret's subsequent passage
over a "stronge brygge" (873) into the earthly paradise
and her marriage to a youthful Christ in a white chapel
are likewise not without precedents. The bridge into
heaven or the earthly paradise is quite common, though
it is usually a "test-bridge," which the virtuous cross
easily and the wicked find treacherously narrow and
impassable.[28] Echoing the marriage of Christ and the
Church in Rev. 19.7, wedding ceremonies are enacted in

---

[27]Os 23.

[28]The first appearance of the bridge in the West
is found in the Dialogues of Pope Gregory the Great and
apparently derives from oriental sources. The
Dialogues of Saint Gregory, trans. and ed. Edmund G.
Gardner (London: Warner, 1911) 223-26; Os 21-22; Patch
95-97.

saints' lives and mystical writings. For example, at
the point of Saint Katherine's martyrdom, Christ
addresses the saint: "Cum, mi leoue leofman;/cum nu,
min iweddet,/leouest an wummon!" and Katherine is
welcomed by the heavenly multitude "with the crown of
conquerors."[29] In Saint Bridget's Revelations Christ
"tellyth seynte Birgitte why he chesyth hyr to be hys
spovse, and how as a spowse she awyth to aray hyr and
be redy to hym."[30] Margery Kempe, likewise, is
spiritually married to God.[31]

Just as A Revelation of Purgatory emphasizes the
concept of purgatory as a place of progressive
purification, it endorses--or, to borrow a phrase,
"propagandizes for"[32]--the prayers, masses, and works
of the faithful on behalf of the souls in purgatory.
While in Drythelm and the Legend of St. Patrick's
Purgatory there are statements endorsing this valuable
intercession, in A Revelation of Purgatory the process
of intercession is enacted. The spirit of Margaret
asks that the visionary request that a total of
thirteen masses be said for her by six priests, whom
she names. The visionary reports that the following

---

[29]The Life of Saint Katherine, ed. E. Einenkel,
EETS os 80 (London, 1884) 119-20.

[30]Revelations of St. Birgitta 1.

[31]The Book of Margery Kempe, ed. Sanford Brown
Meech, prefatory note by Hope Emily Allen, EETS os 212
(London: Oxford UP, 1940) 86-89; see 301 n.86/16 for
references to other such mystical marriages.

[32]Bloomfield 221.

day she visited or sent to all of the priests and that
they granted the request. The question-and-answer
sessions of the visionary and Margaret--exchanges
paralleled in other visions[33]--invite Margaret's
discussions of the special powers of the psalm Miserere
mei deus and the hymn Veni creator spiritus (129ff), as
well as her not entirely consistent analysis of the
relative strengths of the masses (151ff; see
explanatory note 156-59). Characteristic of the
thoroughgoing encouragement of the masses for the
purgatorial souls is Margaret's assurance that, "if
þese masses be seid for any sowle þat is dampned, ȝit
shal þe help and þe mede turne to þe next of his kyn in
purgatory" (164-69; see explanatory note 164-69).

In addition to underscoring the value of the
masses, the vision demonstrates the value of good deeds
performed on behalf of the suffering spirit. The worm
of conscience, in an effort to prevent Margaret's

---

[33]For example, in Guillaume de Deguileville's
Pylgremage of the Sowle, there is a traditional
body-soul debate (fols. 46v-48v). The dialogue element
is an even more conspicuous feature of the
fourteenth-century vision of purgatory The Gast of Gy,
in which Guy's ghost is pressed for answers to a number
of questions about the Christian afterlife. For an
introduction to the work, see Francis Lee Utley,
"Dialogues, Debates, and Catechisms," in A Manual of
the Writings in Middle English: 1050-1500, gen. eds. J.
Burke Severs and Albert E. Hartung, 6 vols. to date
(Hamden, Conn.: Conn. Acad. of Arts and Sciences,
1967-) 3:698-700, 864-65. C. Horstman prints one
manuscript version of The Gast of Gy in Yorkshire
Writers, 2 vols. (New York, 1895) 2:292-333.
Explanatory notes call attention to similarities
between the Gast and the Revelation.

release from purgatory, hopes to weigh against her an unfulfilled promise--her vow to pilgrimage to Southwick--but this obstacle is easily dismissed, for the visionary is presented as one who fulfilled the pledge for Margaret. Thus, Margaret's release from the pains of purgatory is largely effected through the works of the dreamer (who receives the vision, delivers the messages to the six priests, and has previously completed a pilgrimage for Margaret) and through the masses performed by the priests.

In summary, A Revelation of Purgatory is typical of the afterlife literature in its four-part division of the Christian afterlife and in its physical representation of purgatorial torments. Its subdivision of purgatory into three purgatories (one of which is also tripartite) is characteristic of other contemporary revelations and makes possible a graphic representation of the purgatorial spirit's progressive purification. The Revelation generally surpasses the earlier visions in its dramatic endorsement of the efficacious intercession of the living for the souls in purgatory--a belief belonging to the earliest Church teachings.

The Woman Visionary

While its depiction of gradual purgation and its
encouragement of masses to mitigate a soul's suffering
make A Revelation of Purgatory remarkable in content
among the afterlife visions, the circumstances of its
composition likewise distinguish it. Of the seven
Middle English legends of the afterlife that Foster
catalogues in A Manual of the Writings in Middle
English, the Revelation is the latest of the works and
the only one that does not originate in a Latin or
continental version. Of still greater significance is
its genesis in the personal experience of a woman, a
circumstance that ties A Revelation of Purgatory to the
tradition of female visionaries and writers in the
Middle Ages.

Very little literature by women survives from the
Middle Ages. The tenth-century German dramatist
Hrotsvitha, the twelfth-century Anglo-Norman poet Marie
de France, and Christine de Pizan in the early fifteenth century are bright exceptions. Similarly, the
existence of more than a dozen women troubadours in the
twelfth and thirteenth centuries is astonishing, though
the number may appear inconsequential when compared to
the more than four hundred male troubadours. In Middle
English there are no secular works that can for a
certainty be ascribed to women authors. Two short
allegorical poems of the fifteenth century, The Flower
and the Leaf and The Assembly of Ladies, purport to be
by women, but their most recent editor rejects the idea

of female authorship.[34] A few Middle English lyrics
are signed by women, but whether the signatures are
those of composers or scribes remains undecided.

Women writers make greater contributions to
religious literature in the medieval period. Undoubt-
edly, the "most important contribution of women to
spiritual creativity in the Middle Ages was in the
sphere of Christian mysticism": "The great female
mystics were accorded status and respect which no other
women won."[35] A rollcall of the "great female mystics"
might reasonably begin with Hildegard of Bingen (1098-
1179), who "still confronts us, after eight centuries,
as an overpowering, electrifying presence --and in many
ways an enigmatic one."[36] From early childhood Hildegard was "subject to troubling visions"; in 1136, after
assuming the role of abbess at the convent of
Disibodenberg (where she had enrolled as a novice at
age seven), Hildegard "began to record the visions that
had haunted her for years."[37] Other German nuns of

---

[34]Derek A. Pearsall, ed., The Floure and the Leafe
(London: Thomas Nelson, 1962) 14-16. For a
reconsideration of Pearsall's argument, see Ann
McMillan, "'Fayre Sisters Al': The Flower and the Leaf
and The Assembly of Ladies," Tulsa Studies in Women's
Literature 1 (1982): 27-42.

[35]Shulamith Shahar, The Fourth Estate: A History
of Women in the Middle Ages, trans. Chaya Galai (New
York: Methuen, 1983) 56.

[36]Peter Dronke, Women Writers of the Middle Ages
(Cambridge, Eng.: Cambridge UP, 1984) 144.

[37]Frances Gies and Joseph Gies, Women in the
Middle Ages (New York: Crowell, 1978) 63, 76.

recognized importance in the area of female mysticism
are Elizabeth of Schonau (d.1164), a contemporary of
Hildegard, Mechtilde of Magdeburg (1210-97), Mechtilde
of Hackeborn (c.1241-98), and St. Gertrude the Great
(c.1256-1302).   In the fourteenth century, two
outstanding visionaries are St. Bridget of Sweden
(1303-73, canonized 1391) and St. Catherine of Siena
(c.1347-80, canonized 1461).

The women were not only visionaries, but writers
as well. Hildegard's literary production was, among
medieval women, comparatively "vast," to borrow
Dronke's description; in the most widely known of her
works, the Scivias, Hildegard's ideas on "nature, human
physiology, the moral world, the cosmos, the soul" are
"expressed in terms of vision and revelation."[38]
Mechtilde of Magdeburg "wrote lyric poetry of great
beauty,"[39] Gertrude the Great recorded Mechtilde of
Hackeborn's experiences in The Book of Special Grace,
St. Catherine of Siena left her Dialogue, and St.
Bridget wrote her Revelations, "chiefly about Christ's
sufferings and about future events."[40]

In the fourteenth and early fifteenth centuries,
Dame Julian of Norwich (1342-after 1416) and Margery
Kempe (1373-c.1440) emerge to continue the tradition in
England. As one critic observes, "they are the most

---

[38]Gies and Gies 78, 79.

[39]Gies and Gies 86.

[40]Donald Attwater, The Penguin Dictionary of
Saints, 2nd ed., rev. by Catherine Rachel John (1965;
New York: Penguin, 1983) 234, 80, 71.

prominent female <u>writers</u> of Middle English devotional prose, women who break a long tradition of feminine silence in England.'"[41] Julian's revelations survive in a longer and a shorter version, the longer representing a re-vision (twenty years later) of the sixteen "shewings" originally received on 8 May 1373 following a serious illness. By the time she explores and expands her <u>Revelations of Divine Love</u>, Julian is an anchoress enclosed at St. Julian's Church in Norwich. It was there, in fact, that Margery Kempe (likewise from a town in Norfolk) visited the anchoress in the first decade of the fifteenth century, seeking encouragement--and a respected ally. Beyond the more obvious similarities--their common ground of Norfolk, their revelatory illnesses (Margery's first vision and consequent conversion free her from the madness following the birth of her first child)--the two women seem mainly to offer contrasts. Whereas Dame Julian embraces the solitary life, Margery, having negotiated a chastity agreement with her husband John, seeks spiritual satisfaction in her travels throughout England and her pilgrimages to Jerusalem, Rome, and the popular shrine of Santiago de Compostela. Her extravagant displays of affective piety, such as the gift of "the new scream" at the Holy Sepulchre, are without parallel in Julian's recorded experiences. Where Julian's <u>Revelations of Divine Love</u> are ruminative, even intellectual, Margery's autobiography

----

[41]Robert K. Stone, <u>Middle English Prose Style: Margery Kempe and Julian of Norwich</u> (The Hague: Mouton, 1970) 12. Stone cites <u>The Book of Margery Kempe</u> lxii.

--"the first to be written in English,"[42] it is pointed out--is valued as a very entertaining record of an unguarded, exceptional personality and an enlightening witness of late medieval popular piety.

The anonymous woman visionary of A Revelation of Purgatory invites comparisons with her predecessors. I argue below in the section "Date, Origin, and Authorship" that the vision of Margaret's transit through purgatory (received on 10 August 1422 and the two following nights) originated in Winchester in the experiences of a nun of perhaps Nunnaminster (St. Mary's Abbey). The incipit of T refers to the woman as "ane holy woman" (fol. 250v); in L's table of contents, she is termed "a deuout womman solitary" (fol. 2r), and L closes "Explicunt Reuelationes reuelate cuidam sancte mulieri recluse" (fol. 165v). It seems unlikely that the labels "solitary" and "recluse," which come, after all, outside the text, are accurate. The visionary tells us that a little girl rose to pray with her on the first night, and we later learn that on the following morning the visionary went to and sent to the priests of whom Margaret petitioned masses. While perhaps the little girl could have been a servant--a circumstance not unfamiliar to a medieval solitary[43] --the visionary's necessary movements beyond her cell

_____

[42]Louise Collis, Memoirs of a Medieval Woman: The Life and Times of Margery Kempe (1964; New York: Harper, 1983) 9.

[43]Julian of Norwich, Revelations of Divine Love, trans. Clifton Wolters (1968; New York: Penguin, 1984) 23.

(visiting the priests, making a pilgrimage earlier to
Southwick) stretch the terms "solitary" and "recluse"
too far. The possibility that the visionary was not,
like Julian of Norwich, a solitary, but rather an
unallied holy woman more in the manner of Margery Kempe
may merit some consideration. The visionary's second
reference to "a lytel mayd child" (51) is, in fact, to
"my child" (54; emphasis added). But given her
familiarity with a number of Hampshire priests, her
acquaintance with the nun Margaret, and the commonplace
presence of children in nunneries (entered as novices
and students), the visionary was more than likely a
nun, as were so many female visionaries before her.

Whether the unknown visionary merits recognition
as a mystic and a writer remains to be considered.
Since we know nothing of the visionary beyond the
contents of A Revelation of Purgatory, we have no
justification for describing her as a mystic, a term
reserved for those who pursue "a conscious, deep, and
intimate union of the soul with God" through a program
of asceticism and contemplation.[44] The visionary of A
Revelation of Purgatory has a more limited reputation;
she acknowledges that the pains of purgatory have been
shown to her "many tymes before" (14-15), and Margaret
refers to others who "haue appered to þe or þis"
(212-13). In the preceding section of the
introduction, the similarities between the conceptions
of purgatory in A Revelation of Purgatory and a passage

---

[44]Julian of Norwich 25. Also see Richard Rolle,
The Fire of Love, trans. Clifton Wolters (1972; New
York: Penguin, 1981) 21-22.

from St. Bridget's <u>Revelations</u> are pointed out. Both
St. Bridget and Margery Kempe (who sought, unashamedly,
to emulate and surpass St. Bridget) received visions of
the circumstances of souls in purgatory. <u>A Revelation
of Purgatory</u> thus stands as an elaboration of a kind of
vision included in the works of other visionaries.

While there is insufficient support for considering the visionary a mystic, she can reasonably be
termed a writer. The form of <u>A Revelation of Purgatory</u>
is a narrative, one dictated to a priest, a father
confessor in whom the visionary has confided previous
purgatorial visions (15). Of Julian of Norwich's and
Margery Kempe's works, Stone acknowledges that one
might well ask "how much of these writings is actually
the mystics' own?"[45] Admittedly, the relationship
between mystical experiences and their recordings is a
vexed question. Going back to the early Christian
martyr Saint Perpetua (d.203), we find that she recorded in notes the four visions she received while
imprisoned and that the notes were later incorporated
into another writer's work, <u>The Passion of Saints
Perpetua and Felicity</u>.[46] Hildegard dictated a number
of writings, and St. Gertrude's <u>Herald of God's Loving-
Kindness</u> was "mostly written from her notes or dicta-
tion but in part by herself."[47] Many have not taken as
firm proof of Julian of Norwich's illiteracy her

---

[45]Stone 19.

[46]See Dronke 1-16.

[47]Attwater 168, 150.

self-description as "a simple creature that cowde no letter."[48]   Margery Kempe's reliance on two male amanuenses is unquestioned, though the degree of their influence is unsettled.[49]   As Atkinson summarizes, "The relation of author and scribe in this work is complicated and uncertain, but it remains Margery's book, even if the shadowy scribal presence clouds the image in the mirror."[50]   This assessment suggests our final view of the writer of A Revelation of Purgatory. We will no doubt never know whether the speaker's familiarity with the afterlife literature was at points fortified by a collaborative scribe or whether the vision's emphasis on the masses was increased to better serve clerical interests. However, as the visionary graphically narrates to her "gostly fadyr," we sense an authentic voice--in her references to previous showings, in her admissions of fear and isolation, in her earnest questions of the spirit Margaret, and in the often ingenuous imagery of her descriptions of physical torments.

---

[48]Julian of Norwich, A Revelation of Love, ed. Marion Glasscoe (Exeter: U of Exeter, 1976) 2. See Stone 13 n.8.

[49]See Stone 19-23; J. C. Hirsch, "Author and Scribe in The Book of Margery Kempe," Medium Aevum 44 (1975): 145-50; and Clarissa W. Atkinson, Mystic and Pilgrim: The Book and the World of Margery Kempe (Ithaca: Cornell UP, 1984) 28-36.

[50]Atkinson 36.

CRITICAL TEXT

Date, Origin, and Authorship

According to the visionary, the first revelation occurred on "Seynt Lorence Day at ny3t, the 3er of Our Lord M[1]CCCCxxij" (9-10) and was followed by visions on the two following nights. This internal date of 10 August 1422 accords well with the paleographical dating of the three manuscripts, Longleat MS. 29 (L) and the Thornton Manuscript (T) dating from the second quarter of the fifteenth century and Bodleian MS. Eng. th. c. 58 (B) from perhaps the third.[1]

The internal references clearly indicate that the vision originated in Winchester. Six priests are referred to in the Revelation. In commissioning masses of these priests, the purgatorial spirit directs the visionary to "send to" (112; emphasis added) the recluse of Westminster to ask that masses be said,[2] and she asks that the recluse be told to advise Peter Combe (116-17) to perform certain masses. The recluse of Westminster to whom Margaret directs the dreamer has been identified as one of two recluses living at the Benedictine abbey in 1422, John London and William Alnwick. By appointment of King Henry V, William

---

[1]A. I. Doyle, letter, 27 October 1980.

[2]On the "race of Westminster recluses," see David Knowles, The Religious Orders in England, Volume 2: The End of the Middle Ages (Cambridge, Eng.: Cambridge UP, 1955) 219-22.

Alnwick interrupted his confinement at Westminster to become "first confessor-general of the Bridgettines of Twickenham from c.1416/17 to 1418."[3] John London's career is better documented. His activities at Westminster Abbey date from 1378-79 to 1428-29 when he is listed _inter mortuos_.[4] Knowles surmises that John London, "after filling the posts of treasurer of Queen Eleanor's manors and warden of the misericord, had retired into the _reclusorium_ soon after 1390, as the St. Albans annalist implies after recording his death in 1429, after forty years as a hermit."[5] John London is listed among the benefactors of both Westminster Abbey[6] and Syon monastery,[7] and is named in the will of Lord Scrope of Masham in 1415.[8] Though Clay notes that William Alnwick and John London were contemporaries, she identifies the recluse of A Revelation of Purgatory

---

[3]Knowles 367.

[4]E. H. Pearce, The Monks of Westminster (Cambridge, Eng.: Cambridge UP, 1916) 115. I am indebted to Dr. A. I. Doyle for calling this reference to my attention.

[5]Knowles 220.

[6]Arthur P. Stanley, Historical Memorials of Westminster Abbey, 3rd and rev. ed. (London, 1869) 641; cited by Pearce 115 and Clay 112.

[7]Margaret Deanesly, ed., The Incendium Amoris of Richard Rolle of Hampole (London: Longmans, Green, 1915) 124; cited by Knowles 220.

[8]Clay 112, 154; Knowles 220.

as Sir John London.[9] Knowles acknowledges that John London may be "the recluse of Westminster referred to in the Revelation respecting Purgatory of 1422," but he reminds us that William Alnwick is yet "another candidate for the . . . distinction."[10]

The second Westminster priest is Peter Combe, whose duties at the abbey date from 1363.[11] While perhaps Peter Combe's celebrity did not equal that of the Westminster recluse, he too was known as a benefactor of the abbey[12] and was noted for directing the destruction of the tomb of Abbot Richard de Berking (d.1246) during the abbacy of William Colchester (1386-1420).[13] He was listed "inter mortuos 1423-4 . . . so probably died 1422-3."[14]

In contrast to her directions to send to Westminster, Margaret, the purgatorial spirit, directs

---

[9]Clay 154.

[10]Knowles 220.

[11]Pearce 108-09.

[12]Stanley 641; cited by Clay 155 n.1.

[13]John Flete, The History of Westminster Abbey, ed. J. A. Robinson (Cambridge, Eng.: Cambridge UP, 1909) 106; cited by Pearce 109. "[N]othing more is known of Peter Combe's destruction of the tomb of Abbot Richard de Berking. . . . As the chapel in which it stood was itself destroyed in the early 16th century and replaced by the present Henry VII's Chapel, there seems no hope now of establishing what occurred or why." Howard M. Nixon, Librarian, Muniment Room and Library, Westminster Abbey, letter, 2 August 1982.

[14]Pearce 109.

the visionary to "bidde" Master Forest, Sir Richard
Bone, and Don John Pery to say masses for her (97, 121,
125), and further she tells the dreamer to "go to" Sir
John Wynbourne (108; emphasis added). The visionary,
in fact, reports that on the following day she "went
to" Master Forest and Sir John Wynbourne (230, 234;
emphasis added), and she summarily reports that all the
other priests granted the requests.

   All four of the priests accessible to the
visionary are found in Winchester. Master Forest is
John Forest, who received the first of his many
appointments in 1390 and died on 25 March 1446.[15] From
his lengthy list of benefices, which include numerous
concurrent appointments (as canon, prebendary, rector,
etc.), determining his whereabouts on 10 August 1422
would seem a formidable task, but closer inspection and
additional evidence place John Forest in Winchester.
As early as 1405-06 he was treasurer of the household
of Henry Beaufort, Bishop of Winchester (1404-47).[16]
The honorific "Master" is attributable to his position
as Master of the famous St. Cross Hospital, Winchester,
from 1410 to 1444.[17] His concurrent appointment as

---

[15]"Forest, John," in A. B. Emden, A Biographical
Register of the University of Oxford to A.D. 1500
(1957).

   [16]The Register of the Common Seal of the Priory of
St. Swithun, Winchester, 1345-1497, ed. Joan Greatrex,
Hampshire Record Series 2 (n.p.: Hampshire County
Council, 1978) 208, n.3 to item 107.

   [17]For a description of St. Cross, see The Victoria
History of Hampshire, ed. H. Arthur Doubleday and
(Footnote Continued)

rector of Wonston (8 May 1412-14) speaks for his presence in the Winchester area,[18] but more significant is his active role in the affairs of St. Swithun's, the Benedictine priory serving Winchester Cathedral.[19] A lifetime pension granted to him in April 1414 by the priory "for his esteemed counsel and help on many past occasions" suggests that John Forest was a member of the prior's council.[20] In 1417 Bishop Henry Beaufort (by then Cardinal) appointed him his vicar-general, a

---

(Footnote Continued)
William Page, 5 vols. (Westminster: Whitehall, 1900-03; London: Constable, 1908-12) 2:193-97, 5:417-18; also David Knowles and R. Neville Hadcock, Medieval Religious Houses: England and Wales (1953; London: Longmans, Green, 1971) 404. The dates supplied in Victoria 2:197 are 1426-44; Emden alters the first to "By Feb. 1415," offering no termination date. The records of St. Swithun's Priory show that "By March 1410 he was Master of St. Cross" (Register). John Forest was also Master of Godshouse, Portsmouth (1408-still in 1415), likewise in Hampshire (Emden).

[18]Emden supplies the date of appointment, relying on Visitations of Religious Houses, Volume 1: 1420-1436, ed. A. Hamilton Thompson (Horncastle, Eng.: Morton, 1914) 186. Referring to a list of rectors of Wonston, Rev. V. W. Norriss, Rector of Wonston, supplies the resignation date 1414, the time of John Forest's collation to the Archdeaconry of Surrey. Rev. V. W. Norriss, letter, 16 July 1982.

[19]See Victoria 2:108-15 for a brief history of the priory; also Knowles and Hadcock 80-81.

[20]Register 50, item 149; 213, n.1 to item 149. There are further references in the Register to Master Forest as jurist (39-40, item 107) and witness (45, item 126; 46, item 130), and as beneficiary of John Fromond, a "steward of the manors of Winchester College from 1408-20" (214, n.3 to item 153).

4

position he still held in 1425.[21] That John Forest served as Archdeacon of Surrey from 1414 until at least 1422, and possibly until his death,[22] is further evidence of his preeminence in the Winchester diocese at the time of the Revelation.

John Pery and Richard Bone are likewise Winchester priests. Both appear in the ordination records of William Wykeham, Bishop of Winchester (1367-1404). John Pery, a monk of St. Swithun's Priory, graduated from acolyte to subdeacon, deacon, and priest in the years 1387-89.[23] The September 1393 entry in Wykeham's register names Richard Bone among the acolytes in the "city of Winchester"; the subsequent ordinations as subdeacon, deacon, and priest (1393-94) place him in Winchester at Nunnaminster (St. Mary's Abbey).[24]

The fourth priest to whom the visionary goes is John Wynbourne, who, at the time of A Revelation of Purgatory, was the prior of Christchurch-Twynham, a house of Austin canons in the diocese of Winchester.[25]

---

[21]Register 208, n.3 to item 107; Emden.

[22]Emden.

[23]Wykeham's Register, ed. Thomas Frederick Kirby, 2 vols. (London, 1896) 1:315-19; The Compotus Rolls of the Obedientiaries of St. Swithun's Priory, Winchester, ed. G. W. Kitchin (London, 1892) 474. John Pery was among those participating in 1404 in the election of Wykeham's successor as bishop, Henry Beaufort (Register 23-25, item 68).

[24]Wykeham's 1:329-33.

[25]On the Priory of Christchurch-Twynham, see

(Footnote Continued)

Bishop Wykeham's ordination of John Wynbourne as
acolyte, subdeacon, deacon, and priest is recorded
through the years 1393-98.[26] In 1402 John Wynbourne
was one of seven canons who, "animated by a devilish
spirit, entered into a conspiracy" to overthrow the
prior; this "grievous rebellion" culminated in
disciplinary action taken against the canons.[27] The
incident is recalled in 1412 in a papal letter to the
prior of Christchurch-Twynham, mandating absolution for
the offending canons (among them, John Wynbourne) in
response to their petition.[28] Wynbourne's career did
not suffer as a result of this notoriety. In 1416 he
served as the personal chaplain of Thomas Beaufort (d.
1427), Earl of Dorset and brother of Bishop Henry
Beaufort; in a letter of 1416, the prior and convent of
St. Swithun's granted Thomas Beaufort "Confraternity .

(Footnote Continued)
Victoria 2:152-60; also Knowles and Hadcock 154.
Though Victoria supplies no dates for John Wynbourne as
prior, he evidently succeeded Thomas Talbot in 1420 and
was still serving in 1425. Mackenzie E. C. Walcott,
Memorials of Christchurch-Twynham, 3rd ed., rev. by B.
Edmund Ferrey (Christchurch, 1883) 70.

[26]Wykeham's 1:329, 336, 341, 345. The
identification of Wynbourne as one of two "canons of
Tichfield" (345) is an error. The manuscript, in the
keeping of the Hampshire Record Office, Winchester,
identifies Wynbourne, as anticipated, as canon of
Christchurch- Twynham, and Thomas Beel alone is a canon
of Tichfield (fol. 411v).

[27]Victoria 2:157-58; Wykeham's 2:535-36.

[28]Calendar of Entries in the Papal Registers
Relating to Great Britain and Ireland: Papal Letters,
1198-1404, eds. W. H. Bliss and J. A. Twemlow, 6 vols.
(London: Mackie, 1904) 6:282.

. . on account of his special devotion to and affection for them," and Thomas Beaufort's written reply acknowledges that, "His chaplain, sieur John Winbourne . . . informed him of their loving kindness toward him . . . ."[29] John Wynbourne's rise to the position of prior in 1420 doubtless increased his presence in Winchester. In a legal action in 1424, in fact, he is named as a co-executor of the estate of a citizen of Winchester.[30]

Alongside the names of the priests, we are given the Christian name Margaret for the purgatorial spirit but no names at all for the visionary and the priest to whom she relates her dreams. We are told in the Revelation that Margaret "was in hyr lyue a sustre of a house of religious" (43-44; also 90). About the visionary we know that she was a woman experienced in such visions (13-15, 19-20, 212), that she knew the nun Margaret, and that she and Margaret apparently shared the same priests. Her reference to "a lytel mayd child" (51) who rose to pray with her likewise suggests that she was a nun, for "It was a fairly general custom among the English nuns . . . to receive children for education," and one "habit against which bishops constantly legislated was that of having the children

---

[29]Register 58, items 173 and 174.

[30]Calendar of the Patent Rolls Preserved in the Public Record Office: Henry IV, 1422-1429 (Norwich: Norfolk Chronicle, 1901) 238.

to sleep in the dorter with the nuns," an "exceedingly
common" practice.[31]

That the four priests are found in Winchester
argues strongly that the purgatorial spirit Margaret
and the visionary with her were nuns at one of the
three Benedictine houses in the Winchester area,
Romsey, Wherwell, and Nunnaminster (St. Mary's
Abbey).[32] Because Wherwell and Romsey are ten miles to
the northwest and southwest of Winchester, Nunnaminster
is the clearest choice. That John Pery was a monk of
St. Swithun's suggests Nunnaminster, since the priory
and abbey had a history of contact,[33] and Richard
Bone's position as priest at Nunnaminster supplies even
more convincing support.

Nunnaminster, in fact, accommodates the particulars of the Revelation quite well. In addition to an
abbess, twenty-six nuns, thirteen poor sisters, and
several priests, the relatively large abbey housed (at
the time of the Dissolution) twenty-six children of

---

[31]Eileen Power, Medieval English Nunneries (1922;
New York: Biblo and Tannen, 1964) 261, 273.

[32]On the three houses, see Victoria 2:126-32,
132-37, 122-26; also Knowles and Hadcock 264, 267, 268.

[33]"Bishops and Councils constantly forbade nuns to
frequent houses of monks, or to be received there as
guests, but the practice continued. Sometimes they had
an excuse; the nuns of St. Mary's, Winchester, were in
the habit of going to St. Swithun's monastery to
confess to one of the brothers, who was their confessor
and in ill-health, and Bishop Pontoise [1282-1304]
appointed another monk in his place, thus avoiding the
risk of scandal" (Power 387).

noble birth.[34] And there was no dearth of Margarets at
Nunnaminster; among thirteen novices inducted at St.
Mary's on 12 September 1400 are the Margarets
Tycheborne, Wodelok, Werkman, and Vowell.[35] Finally,
because the Revelation shows clear familiarity with
other visionary works, the exceptional presence of a
librarian in 1501 may be significant, implying as it
does a commitment to religious literature at the
abbey.[36]

    Thus, while the Revelation fails to reveal the
name of its author--the visionary, in fact, inadver-
tently teases us with her recollection, "sho . . .
named my name" (220-21, 642)--we are given sufficient
details to identify the work, with some confidence, as
a product of Winchester's Nunnaminster, and one that
sheds light on the religious life of Winchester and the
county of Hampshire. The Revelation brings together
religious men and women of three long-standing
Winchester institutions, Nunnaminster, St. Swithun's,
and the Hospital of St. Cross. Just as the mention of
John Wynbourne brings Christchurch-Twynham into the
sphere of reference, the allusion to the pilgrimage to
Southwick (822) extends the topographical references to
include another house of Austin canons, Southwick

---

[34]Victoria 2:122; Power 151; Knowles and Hadcock
268.

[35]Wykeham's 2:519.

[36]Power 241 n.4. On Nunnaminster's library, see
Medieval Libraries of Great Britain, ed. N. R. Ker, 2nd
ed. (London: Royal Historical Society, 1964) 201-02.

Priory, where the shrine to Our Lady was located.[37]
These references to persons and places, which doubtless
deepened the interest for a contemporary audience,
reduce our sense of the anonymity of the author and
increase our appreciation of the vision as an authentic
personal expression of early fifteenth-century popular
belief about the Christian afterlife.

---

[37]Victoria 2:164-68; also Knowles and Hadcock 174.
"Southwik is a good bigge thorough fare but no
celebrate market. The fame of it stode by the priory
of the Blake Chanons there and a pilgrimage to Our
Lady." John Leland, The Itinerary, Parts I-III, ed.
Lucy Toulmin Smith, 5 vols. (1907; Carbondale:
Southern Illinois UP, 1964) 1:284.

The Manuscripts

Descriptions

(L)   Longleat MS. 29, held in the library of the
Marquess of Bath at Longleat in Warminster, dates from
the second quarter of the fifteenth century.[38]   A
manuscript of 169 vellum leaves, L is a religious
miscellany containing Latin and English works.[39]   In
addition to the incomplete, unascribed version of
Chaucer's Parson's Tale (fols. 81r-128v), L contains
Walter Hilton's De Vita Activa et Contemplativa (fols.
58v-69r)[40] and works by Richard Rolle.[41] A Revelation
of Purgatory, or "a notable reuelacion of þe peyns of
purgatory shewed to a deuout womman solitary" (fol.
2r), is the last work in the miscellany (fols.
155r-165v).

---

[38]Doyle. The Parson's Tale in L (fols. 81r-128v)
is dated 1420-30 in John M. Manly and Edith Rickert,
The Text of the Canterbury Tales, 8 vols. (Chicago: U
of Chicago P) 1:345. As Manly and Rickert note, the
poems on fols. 143v-146v, "Myghtefful Mari y-crownyd
quene," "Off mercy quene & emperesse," and "Timor
mortis conturbat me," are later additions to the
manuscript.

[39]Manly and Rickert's description includes a list
of the contents. The manuscript itself supplies a
table of contents at fol. 2r.

[40]Manly and Rickert give fols. 58v-73v, but
69r-73v are folios of "A Tretice to Lerne How a Man
Shal Suffre Desaises & Not Despeir."

[41]The works by Rolle in L are discussed by Allen
34-36.

As Manly and Rickert note, L is comprised of four books. Book four (fols. 147r-169v), which contains A Revelation of Purgatory, is made up of three gatherings: 1^8, 2^9 (i added), 3^4. If the third gathering is lacking i, ii, vii, and viii, as Manly and Rickert suggest, the four folios were lost prior to the transcription of A Revelation of Purgatory, since the piece begins the second gathering at fol. 155r and continues without defect through the first two folios of the third gathering.

The leaf size is 207 x 153 mm, the writing space 160 x 110 mm. There is marginal ruling, with 30-34 lines of text per page in A Revelation of Purgatory.

The ink is generally brown but varies to black occasionally. Red ink is used for headnotes, capitula, underlining, and initials. At the top of fol. 155r L has the headnote "Reuelacio notabilis," preceded by a capitulum. The word "notabilis" reappears at the top of fol. 156r, and again, preceded by the capitulum, as a headnote to fols. 157r and 158r. A single capitulum recurs at the top of all other folio pages through fol. 161r. There are ten simple initials in the text, each two lines in height.

The script in A Revelation of Purgatory is a typical anglicana. Distinctive letters are the double-lobed a (with single-compartment secretary a a rare exception); broken-circle e; figure-8 g; long r and 2-shaped r (with short secretary r showing up only in the word ar); sigma s (though the 6- or small B-shaped final s of secretary is frequent); and the circular lobed w. Thorns, distinguishable from y, and yoghs are frequent.

Allen reports only that L's texts are "not Northern,"[42] and Manly and Rickert's analysis of L's dialect is likewise indecisive: "Although most of the texts are Northern in origin, few traces of the Northern dialect remain; . . . it seems impossible to locate the scribe definitely. He may have been of a Central Midland region."[43] In 1968, however, Angus McIntosh and M. L. Samuels included L in their "handlist of mediaeval Anglo-Irish documents and texts."[44] Relying on localized and partially localized documents, as well as on "Unlocalized texts dealing with Irish matters or having other Irish associations, the language of which confirms that provenance," McIntosh and Samuels identify L as one of ten "Unlocalized texts for which the evidence of Irish provenance is wholly or mainly linguistic."[45]

On the basis of the interpretation of a name on fol. 168r as "Joh[s] Goldew[e?]ll," Manly and Rickert trace the provenance of L from the Goldwell family of Canterbury. John Thynne, whose name appears on fols. 2r and 166r, purchased the site of Longleat House in 1541 and is the ancestor of the Marquess of Bath who

---

[42]Allen 34.

[43]Manly and Rickert 346.

[44]"Prolegomena to a Study of Mediaeval Anglo-Irish," Medium Aevum 36 (1968): 1.

[45]McIntosh and Samuels 3. Michael Benskin's more recent work on L and medieval Hiberno-English has led to a tentative assessment of the manuscript as "MHE in language, possibly of Dublin; the MS. plausibly put together in that city." Letter, 20 June 1985.

built Longleat. Though Manly and Rickert argue that L came to John Thynne through descendants of the Goldwells, they acknowledge the possibility (though, indeed, it seems the probability) that John Thynne acquired the manuscript from "his uncle, William Thynne, who collected MSS from various monasteries at the time of the Dissolution."[46]

(T)   Manuscript 91 in the Lincoln Cathedral Library is more commonly known as the Thornton Manuscript, after its scribe, identified as the Robert Thornton of East Newton who "was alive in 1456 but dead by 1465."[47] In the introduction to the facsimile edition, Owen suggests the composition date "c. 1430-50."[48] T is an anothology of secular, religious, and medical writings. Among its secular works are the Morte Arthure and the romances of Octovyane, Sir Degrevante, and Sir Percyvelle of Gales.[49] As Allen notes, T shares with L works by Richard Rolle and Walter Hilton.[50] The medical treatise in the Thornton

---

[46]Manly and Rickert 347-48.

[47]Brewer and Owen viii. For a discussion of T "as a document of literary, cultural, and intellectual history," see George R. Keiser, "Lincoln Cathedral Library MS. 91: Life and Milieu of the Scribe," Studies in Bibliography 32 (1979): 158-79.

[48]Brewer and Owen xvi.

[49]For a complete list of the sixty-four items in T, see Brewer and Owen xvii-xx. On the romances, see J. O. Halliwell, The Thornton Romances (London, 1844).

[50]Allen 36.

Manuscript, the Liber de Diversis Medicinis, is a
compendium of medieval medical practice, including, for
example, recipes for herbal remedies and a tract on the
plague.[51]

Owen observes that T "consisted originally of
around 335 paper leaves, averaging 291 x 210 mm."[52]
The collation of the manuscript reveals seventeen
gatherings of varying sizes. A Revelation of Purgatory
originally comprised the final four folios of the
fourteenth gathering and the first five of the
fifteenth. The "collation confirms" what comparison of
T with L indicates--"that one leaf but no more is lost
between fos. 253 and 254."[53] Allen aptly suggests that
the missing leaf (the first leaf in the fifteenth
gathering) was in all likelihood purposely removed,
containing as it did harsh descriptions of the
purgatorial torments of priests.[54]

There are 34-39 lines of text per page in A
Revelation of Purgatory. The text begins in the middle
of fol. 250v with the indented headnote: "Hic incipit

---

[51]Margaret S. Ogden, ed., The Liber de Diversis
Medicinis in the Thornton Manuscript, EETS os 207
(1938; London: Oxford UP, 1969).

[52]Brewer and Owen xiii. Sarah M. Horrall provides
an analysis of the watermarks in "The Watermarks of the
Thornton Manuscripts," Notes and Queries ns 27 (1980):
385-86.

[53]A. E. B. Owen, "The Collation and Descent of the
Thornton Manuscript," Transactions of the Cambridge
Bibliographical Society 6 (1975): 221.

[54]Allen 36 n.1.

quedam reuelacio, a reuelacyon schewed to ane holy
woman now one late tyme." The text concludes with the
words "Explicit tractatus de visione" in the middle of
fol. 258r. A red initial A̲, five lines in height,
begins the text. There are catchwords at fols. 250v,
253v, 254r, 254v, 255r, 255v, 256v, and 257v. The ink
is brown.

Brewer describes the script of T as "a fairly
typical mid-fifteenth-century cursive hand, vari-
able."[55] His description echoes that found in the New
Palaeographical Society's note, where the handwriting
is described as "at best a carelessly formed cursive
type of script."[56] More specifically, Robert Thornton's hand is an anglicana. With the exception of an
occasional single-bowled a̲, there are no distinctively
secretary graphs. However, Thornton's script is, like
secretary, more angular than typical anglicana. Yoghs
are infrequent, and thorn is indistinguishable from y̲.

The Thornton Manuscript represents a dialect
translation into Robert Thornton's Northern dialect,
the features of which are well represented. The
presence of several o̲ spellings for OE a̲, as in s̲m̲o̲t̲e̲
and t̲w̲o̲, is evidence, in Brewer's words, of "a
different underlying dialect."[57]

---

[55]Brewer and Owen vii.

[56]E. M. Thompson et al., The New Palaeographical
Society: Facsimiles of Ancient Manuscripts, Second
Series (1913-14), notes to plate 45; cited in Brewer
and Owen xv-xvi.

[57]Brewer and Owen vii.

On the provenance of the manuscript, Brewer suggests in his introduction that T was acquired for Lincoln Cathedral Library from the Thornton family "by Michael Honywood, Dean of Lincoln 1660-81."[58] Owen expands on this conjecture, suggesting that T was passed to Honywood by Thomas Comber (1645-99), who had married into the Thornton family.[59] George R. Keiser has since argued that Comber passed the manuscript to Lincoln Cathedral Library not through Honywood but through "his successor, Daniel Brevint, Dean of Lincoln from 1682 to 1695."[60]

(B)   Bodleian MS. Eng. th. c. 58, a manuscript of 28 leaves, is the latest of the three manuscripts, dating from perhaps the third quarter of the fifteenth century.[61] The binding of vellum-covered pasteboard and a calfskin spine is of the eighteenth century. The four gatherings of B--1^5 (wants i, iv, v), 2^7 (wants vii), 3^8, 4^8--contain fragments of three works:[62]

1. Fols. 1r-10r are drawn from chapters 40-47 of The Mirrour of the Blessed Lyf of Jesu Christ, Nicholas

---

[58]Brewer and Owen viii.

[59]A. E. B. Owen 224.

[60]"A Note on the Descent of the Thornton Manuscript," Transactions of the Cambridge Bibliographical Society 6 (1976): 346.

[61]Doyle.

[62]General identification of the contents of B is courtesy of Mr. David Vaisey, Keeper of Western Manuscripts, Bodleian Library, Oxford.

Love's Middle English translation of the Latin
Meditationes Vitae Christi, a work formerly attributed
to St. Bonaventure though not his.[63]   Fols. 1r-2v are
from chapter 40 (219-25 in Powell's edition), beginning
"he prayth to the ffadyr mekely" and ending "but in
maner as herbefor I was wont to do at." Fols. 3r-10r
are from chapters 41-57 (231-53 in Powell's edition),
beginning "of blode and so they scornyd hym" and ending
"went forth har way in prayer and blissid talkyng. And
thus endyth the blyssid passion of Owre Lorde Ihu
Cryst."

    2. Fols. 10r-12v are a fragment of A Revelation
of Purgatory. The piece begins "Almaner thyng that is
begon that may twrne to profite of manes sowle"; fol.
11v ends "And yet or scho went frome me scho saide I
schull se hyr to-nyght in." Between fols. 11 and 12 a
leaf is missing; fol. 12r begins "And therein they cast
hir," and fol. 12v ends "parid of her crownes and hit
semyd to me also her," with the catchwords "fyngris and
her." The headnote of the versos of fols. 10, 11, and
12 is, "Rede, vndyrstand what is to drede."   The
headnote at fols. 11r and 12r reads, "The bettyr lyf
thow myghtest lede."

---

[63]The Mirrour of the Blessed Lyf of Jesu Christ,
ed. Lawrence F. Powell (Oxford: Oxford UP, 1908).
"Notable Accessions," The Bodleian Library Record 2
(1941-49): 169-70 erroneously identifies the piece as
"Meditations on the Passion of Christ, by Ps. Bona-
ventura."

3. The final two gatherings of the manuscript are from chapters 6-31 of <u>The Three Kings of Cologne</u>.[64] Fol. 13r begins "he yede into that contray" (20, line 10 in Horstman's edition), and fol. 28v ends "as to her gostly fadyr the wyche man also," with the catchwords "in the wyche fayth of Cryst."

The leaf size is 310 x 230 mm, and the writing space 218 x 145 mm. There is marginal and linear ruling, with 40 long lines of text per page. The ink is brown; there are simple blue initials, and occasionally red ink is used. In <u>A Revelation of Purgatory</u> the prologue (1-6) is in red ink, as are the titles of hymns and masses, and the text of the vision begins with a blue initial.

The script of <u>A Revelation of Purgatory</u> is a secretary script with some anglicana forms. Distinctive secretary letters are the single-lobed, pointed <u>a</u>; single-lobed, crossed-<u>y</u> <u>g</u>; final small <u>B</u>-shaped s; and <u>w</u> resembling two <u>v</u>'s. The <u>v</u>-shaped secretary <u>r</u> is absent; <u>2</u>-shaped <u>r</u> follows minims and lobed letters, and long <u>r</u> is often used. Anglicana <u>a</u>, <u>g</u>, <u>w</u>, and broken-circle <u>e</u> are used, though infrequently. The yogh is not used; thorns are rare, occasionally found at the right margin. Capital letters, especially <u>A</u>, <u>P</u>, and <u>S</u>, are used inconsistently.

According to McIntosh, the language of the B scribe "cannot be farther North . . . than the South

---

[64]Ed. C. Horstman, EETS os (1886; New York: Kraus, 1973).

Midland area"[65]--a circumstance in accord with the
origin of the piece in Winchester and the association
of the manuscript with Bath and Wells in the late
fifteenth century.

The earliest known owner of the manuscript is
William Squyer. A note on a strip of paper pasted into
the inside of the front cover reads, "Upon the cover of
the Old English Life of Christ was written, Iste liber
constat Wilelmo Squyer.'" This information, supplied
by a later owner (perhaps Thomas Martin, mentioned
below), is confirmed by two marginal notations in the
manuscript: at fol. 11r, the name "Squyer" is found in
the right margin, while the left margin of fol. 28v
bears the name "William." William Squyer, admitted in
1470 as a fellow at All Souls College, Oxford,[66] was
active in the diocese of Bath and Wells, Somerset,
throughout the last decade of the fifteenth century and
well into the sixteenth, serving successively as vicar
of Pennard, rector of Treborough, vicar of Bradford,
official of the archdeacon of Taunton (1517), and vicar
of Wellington (by 1524-still in 1536). The manuscript
later came into the possession of Thomas Martin
(1697-1771), or "Honest Tom Martin of Palgrave" as he
wished to be remembered.[67] The name "Tho. Martin"
appears in the upper lefthand corner of the inside of
the front cover. The manuscript may have come to

---

[65]Angus McIntosh, letter, 26 May 1985.

[66]"Squyer, William," in Emden.

[67]Thompson Cooper, "Martin, Thomas," DNB (1896).

Martin through his marriage to the widow of Peter le
Neve (1661-1729), a notable book-collector for whom
Martin had served as executor.[68] The dispersal of
Martin's collection began in 1769 and continued in a
series of sales following his death in 1771. The
manuscript was temporarily owned by John Ives
(1751-76),[69] a "principal purchaser" of the Martin
collection; pasted onto the front cover of the
manuscript is a small slip bearing the identifying
number 477 from the sale of John Ives's collection in
March 1777. The inside cover also bears the armorial
bookplate of John Borthwick of Crookston.[70] The
manuscript came to the Bodleian Library through
Sotheby's sale on 3 June 1946, which included the
property of Major J. H. S. Borthwick of Borthwick. Lot
210, B was among twenty lots bearing the Borthwick
bookplate, a few of which also bore the bookplate of
John Ives.[71]

---

[68]See Walter Rye, "Le Neve, Peter," DNB (1896);
William Younger Fletcher, English Book Collectors
(London: Paul, Trench, Trubner, 1902) 147-49; and
Seymour de Ricci, English Collectors of Books and
Manuscripts, 1530-1930, and Their Marks of Ownership
(Cambridge, Eng.: Cambridge UP, 1930) 65.

[69]Thompson Cooper, "Ives, John," DNB (1896).

[70]"John Borthwick of Crookston and Borthwick, Co.
Edinburgh" is listed in W. Carew Hazlitt, A Roll of
Honour (London, 1908) 23.

[71]Sotheby and Company, Catalogue of Fine
Illuminated Manuscripts, Valuable Printed Books,
Autograph Letters, and Historical Documents (London:
n.p., 1946).

Manuscript Affiliations

A discussion of the relationships among the three manuscripts L, T, and B may begin with W. W. Greg's clear account of "the ambiguity of three texts":

> . . . where three manuscripts only are concerned, no merely formal process can throw light on the relationship between them. Either the readings will be all divergent or else the variants will be of type 1 [A:BC, B:AC, C:AB], and since, in the latter case, the reading of the single divergent manuscript may always (theoretically at least) be unoriginal, it will never be possible to establish a common source for any pair of manuscripts to the exclusion of the third. Given three manuscripts, therefore, it is impossible either to prove or to disprove independent derivation.[72]

Though admittedly it will be impossible to prove a particular genealogical relationship among the three texts, we can significantly reduce the number of potential relationships by identifying readings in which one of the three manuscripts has a clear error of omission, and we can suggest the more probable stemma

---

[72]W. W. Greg, The Calculus of Variants (Oxford: Clarendon P, 1927) 21.

by examining a few sets of variants involving
agreements in error.

The following three sets of variant readings
involving evident omissions disprove any stemma
involving the immediate descent of one extant
manuscript from another:

     L: whiche wer showed to me many tymes before
     T: whilke was schewed me many tyms by-fore
     B: ther-of   (14-15)

     L: þer came out sparkles of fyr, and out at
        hyr mouth come an
     T: owte of that wonde come
     B: ther came sparkis ovt of fire and also
        out of hyr movth come a   (63-64)

     L: forsaid
     T: als I have saide vn-to the
     B: as I haue seide vnto the ende   (187)

Omissions, however, cannot serve to disprove stemma
where an inferential manuscript intercedes, since
theoretically x could supply any words or lines omitted
from the ancestor. The descent of any two manuscripts
from the third, via one inferential manuscript, is
implausible due to at least three factors: the incom-
pleteness of T and B, the paleographical dating of B,
and the clear errors of homoeoteleuton that T shows L
to contain at 252-53, 723-24, and 774-93.

While admittedly we cannot "prove or disprove
independent variation," the three sets of variants
(drawn from the lines that L, T, and B preserve in

common) arguably involve agreements in error and
suggest as the more probable stemma,

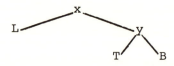

First, at 30 L omits the negative in the
hyperbole, reading "al þe creatures in the world my t
telle þe wikked smyllynge þer-of." Both T and B supply
the negative "neuer"/"nevyr" before the infinitive. I
interpret "neuer" as y's reading, an error shared by T
and B, and introduce "noȝt" as the probable reading of
x. The loss of "noȝt" in "myȝt noȝt," an instance of
haplography,[73] is a likely scribal error, while
"neuer," "an emphatic negative,"[74] would be an
understandable substitution by a scribe copying a
hyperbole in such a necessarily exaggerated text as A
Revelation of Purgatory.[75]

---

[73]The haplography here is an error resulting from
the "optical illusion" caused by the similarity of the
two adjacent words. Anthony G. Petti, English Literary
Hands from Chaucer to Dryden (Cambridge, Mass.:
Harvard UP, 1977) 30.

[74]Tauno F. Mustanoja, A Middle English Syntax,
Mémoires de la Société Néophilologique de Helsinki 23
(Helsinki: Société Néophilologique, 1960) 340.

[75]In his discussion of the habits of the A-text
scribes of Piers Plowman, George Kane observes that,
"In general scribes set out to produce what seemed to
them a more correct, or a more easily intelligible, or
a more emphatic, or a more elegant text"; he further
asserts that "the most striking of the variations
originating from the scribe's association of himself
(Footnote Continued)

Second, the readings at 12 are

    L: fadyr
    T: so
    B: furthermor

Given the frequent repetition of the address "fadyr" in the opening lines of the text, L is the anticipated reading. Evidently, y altered the reading of x from "fadyr" to the similar adverb "further," an alteration explaining the adverbial readings in T and B.

A third set of variants that may support this stemma occurs at 167:

        L: ham out of har purgatory

            yam
        T: hym owte of yaire purgatorie

        B: hym out ther-of

The plural pronouns are grammatically incorrect, since the antecedent is singular. Assuming L preserves the reading of x, it is arguable that y altered the first pronoun to "hym" the reading of B and the original reading of T. The second plural pronoun in the phrase

---

(Footnote Continued)
with what he copied are those designed to increase the emphasis of statements." In fact, Kane includes in his illustrative examples the alteration of "not" to "neuer" in MS. A at line 258. George Kane, ed., Piers Plowman: The A Version (London: Athlone P, 1960) 128, emphasis added; 138, 139.

could have provoked the T scribe to alter "hym" to
"þam" and prompted the B scribe to remedy the
contradiction in number by introducing the adverb
"ther-of." The changes in T and B make it probable
that T and B were copied from a text with this
combination of singular and plural pronouns.

In sum, the variants at 30, 12, and 167 supply the
support for this stemma, and I find no other variants
showing agreement in error between L and B or between L
and T, which would suggest another stemma to challenge
independent derivation.

Editorial Method

The text comes from L, an early manuscript, which, unlike T and B, is without serious physical defects. The spelling of L is retained in the edited text with the exception I, which becomes I or J according to modern spelling. The printed text preserves þ and ȝ; u and v are unaltered, and long i is recorded as j. Punctuation and capitalization are normalized in this edition.

Contractions and suspensions are silently expanded in the text and conform to the spelling of L; the edited text always expands the ampersand of L. Except in abbreviations of numbers, L's supralinear letters (t, u, e, and i) are printed on line, whether they appear in expanded contractions (þat, þou) or in words involving no omission (þe, þi). Latin words and phrases are italicized, with abbreviations silently expanded.

My treatment of the word division of L represents a compromise. Where L separates words now commonly written as one, I join them with a hyphen. A small number of falsely joined words in L are silently separated in the edited text. A virgule in the printed text denotes the beginning of a new page of the manuscript, identified by folio number in the right margin.

All emendations of L are indicated in the edited text. L is emended where its scribe has miswritten words, unintentionally omitted or repeated words, or produced readings that contradict the obvious sense of the text. When I exclude in the printed text words from L, I signal the editorial omission by a supralinear plus sign in the text and record the omission in the Table of Variants. Square brackets surround substitutions or additions of letters or words. With the exception of the bracketed passage (774-93), which is taken from T without alteration, readings from T or B introduced into L are made to conform with the spelling and grammar of L, and the full variant readings of L, T, and B are given in the apparatus.

The method for recording manuscript variants is described at the beginning of the Table of Variants that follows the Middle English text.

The Text

Al maner thynge þat is begon þat may turne to   155r
profite of mannys soule, to God al only be þe
wyrship ȝevyn and to non erthly man ne womman. Der
brether and sustres, al þat reden þis tretis,
lustneth and hireth how a womman was trauallet in   5
hir slep with a spirite of purgatory and how sho
made hir compleynt to hyr gostly fadyr:
    My der fadyr, I do ȝow to witte how grete
tribulacion I hadde in my slep vp-on Seynt Lorence
Day at nyȝt, the ȝer of Our Lord MlCCCCxxij. I   10
went to my bedde at viij of the clok and so I fel
on slep. And fadyr, betwix ix and x me thoght I
was rauyshed into purgatory, and sodeynly I saw al
þe peynes whiche wer showed to me many tymes
before--as ȝe, fadyr, knew wel by my tellynge.   15
Bot sir, I was noȝt shewed by no such spirite þe
syȝt of ham on þis nyȝt of Seynt Lorence. Bot
sodeynly, fadyr, me þoȝt I saw ham, and forsoth,
fadyr, I was neuer so yuel ferd when I woke for
shewynge of þe peynes as I was þan, and þe cause   20
was þat I was ledde by no spirit þat I knewe
byfore þat myȝt haue comforted me.
    And in þis syȝt of purgatory me thoȝt I saw
thre grete fyres, and me þoȝt þat euery fyr was at
oþer end. Bot sir, þer was no departynge betwene   25
ham, bot eueryon eched to oþer. And þese þre
fyres weren wonderful and horrible, and specialy
þe most of al, ffor þat fyr was so horrible and
stynkynge þat al þe creatures in the world myȝt
[noȝt] telle þe wikked smyllynge þer-of. Ffor þer   30

was pych and tarr, lede and brynstone, oyl and al
maner of thynge þat myȝt brenne, and al maner
peynes þat man couth þynk, and al maner Cristen
men and wommen þat lyved her in this world, of
what degre þay wer.   35

Bot amonge al þe peynes / þat I sawe of al   155v
men and wommen, me thoȝt prestes þat had bene
lecherous in har lyfes, and har wommen with
ham--wheþer þay wer religious men and wommen or
seculers--men and wommen of ordyr me thoȝt in þat   40
syȝt þay had moste peyne. And in þat grete fyr me
þoȝt I saw þe spirite of a womman þat I knew
before, þe whiche was in hyr lyue a sustre of a
house of religious, þe which womman whils sho
lyved was called Margaret, whiche me thoȝt I saw   45
in this horrible fyr and had so grete peynes þat
for drede I myȝt noȝt discreue ham at þat tyme.

And in a dredeful feerdnes I wok. And by þat
tyme hit smot þe hour of ten befor mydnyȝt, and
for drede and ferdnesse to slep agayne, I rose vp,   50
and a lytel mayd child with me, and we two seiden
þe vij psallmes and þe lytany. And by we had seid
out Agnus dei, I was so heuy of slep I myȝt noȝt
mak an end, bot bade my child go to bedde, and so
did I. And by þat tyme hit smote xj, and by I had   55
told þe last stroke, I began to slep.

And as fast cam to me þe spirite me thoȝt of
þis womman Margaret, þe whiche I saw before in
peynes, and me þoȝt sho was ful of strange
wou[n]des as she had bene drawen with cambes. And   60
so me þoȝt sho was woundet and rent, bot specialy
at hyr hert me þoȝt I saw a greuous and an

horrible wound; and þer came out sparkles of fyr,
and out at hyr mouth come an flaume of fyr.

And she seid, "Cursed mot þou be and wo worth   65
the bot þou hast þe to be my help."

And me þoȝt by she had seid þe word I was so
ferd I myȝt nat speke, bot euer I þoȝt in my hert,
"Jesus Passion be my help," and with þat I was
comforted in my spirite. And þen me þoȝt sho wold   70
haue cast fyr on me and stert to me to haue slayne
me, bot me þoȝt sho had no power, ffor þe Passion
of God conforted me, bot þe grisly syȝt of hyr
affrayed me. And me þoȝt sho had a / lytel hound   156r
and a lytel catte folwynge hyr, al of fyr   75
brennynge.

And þen me thoȝt I seid to hyr, "Whate art
þou, in Goddis name, þat þus sore trauaillest me?
And I coniur þe in þe Faderes name and þe Son and
þe Holy Gost, þre persons in on God in Trenyte,   80
þat þou tel me what þou art þat þus trauaillest me
and wheþer þou be a spirite of purgatory to haue
help of me oþer a spirite of helle to ouercome me
and trowble me."

And sho seid, "Nay, I am a spirite of   85
purgatory þat wold haue help of the and noȝt a
spirite of helle to drech the. And if þou wil
witte what spirite I am þat suffre grete peynes in
purgatory for my syn, I am þe spirite of Margaret
þat was suster in a susters house of religiouse as   90
þou knowest þat I dwelled þer-in. And in þe name
of God I ask help of þe."

And I asked hyr whate I shold do, and þan sho
seid, "Thou shalt make to be seid for me xiij
masses in the maner as I shal tel þe." And þan   95

sho named a good mannys name, þe which was and is
my confessour.   "And bidde hym say a masse of
Requiem for me, and he shal say v dayes al þis
psalme Miserere⁺ mei deus.   And when he begynneth
to say Miserere mei deus, say he þis vers fyue   100
tymes Miserere mei and þan al out to þe end with
castynge vp hert and eyghen to Godward, ffor þe
more deuoutly he seith hit, pe more relecet shold
be [my] peynes and þe grettyr shold be his mede.
And when he hath seid þis vers⁺ v tymes, let hym   105
say out þe psalme.   And bid hym say þis ympne Veni
creator v dayes.

"Also, go to þy gostly fadyr, Sir John, and
bid hym say for me iij masses of þe Trenyte and
Miserere mei v dayes with þis ympne Veni creator   110
and so forth in þe maner as hit is seid before.

"And also, send to þi fadyr, þe recluse of
Westmyster, and bid hym synge iij masses of Seynt
Peter for me and v dayes þis psalme Miserere and
þis ympne Veni creator and so forth in þe maner   115
afor-seid.   /   And bidde hym warne Don [Petrus] 156v
Combe þat he say two masses of þe Holy Gost for me
and iij dayes þis psalme Miserere mei deus in
maner aforsaid and this ympne Veni creator
spiritus and so forth.   120

"And bidde Sir Richard Bone say two masses of
Our Lady, Salue sancta parens, and iij dayes þis
psalme Miserere and þis ympne Veni creator as hit
is aboue-said.

"And bidde Don John Pery say two masses of Al   125
Seyntes, Gaudeamus, and iij memories of þe Trenite
and iij dayes þis psalme Miserere and þis ympne
Veni creator as hit is aforseid."

And þan I asked hyr why sho desyred þis, to
aske þese masses to be seid in this maner, and sho   130
said þer was no prayer þat my3t raþer help hyr.
And I asked why sho desyred þis psalme <u>Miserere</u> to
be said so ofte for hyr, and sho said for to haue
þe mercy and þe pitte of Almyghty God, ffor als
ofte, sho said, as þat psalme with þis ympne <u>Veni</u>   135
<u>creator</u> bene seid for hyr, so many   peynes sho
shold be relessed of at þat tyme. And also, sho
seid what man or womman þat vseth to   say þis
psalme with þis ympne aboue-seid, yf he be in dowt
of syn or dispeyr of feith or of þe mercy of God,   140
he shal þrogh þe my3t of God haue trew knowlech of
this defaut and þrogh þe mercy of God be delyuered
of þat temptacion as for þe tyme. Also, if man or
womman be tempted in any of þe vij dedely synnys,
as in thefte, manslaghter, sclaundrynge, bakby-   145
tynge, or any cursed syn of lechery, let hym say
with a good hert þese wordes, <u>Miserere</u> <u>mei</u> <u>deus</u>,
and þe ympne <u>Veni</u> <u>creator</u> al   out. þe   wikked
spirits þat trauaillen hym to þat temptacion shal
be voidet at þat tyme.   150

     I asked what profite hit was to a soule to
say more masses of þe Trenyte and of Our Lady and
of Seynt Peter þan hit was of Requiem, and she
said 3is, ther was no-þynge so mych of profite for
a soule-- / who-so wer of power for to do   157r
hit--[as] ffor to mak to be seid for a soule an C   156
masses of the Trenite and an C of Our Lady and l
of Seynt Peter and C of Requiem and half   an
hondred tymes to al þese masses to say <u>Miserere</u>
and <u>Veni</u> <u>creator</u>. And what maner of syn þat he   160
had done in hys live, þer shal no maner of peyne

in purgatory hold hym þat ne hastily he shal be
delyuered from ham and many ⁺other sowlys be
delyuered for his sake. Bot if þese masses be
seid for any sowle þat is dampned, ȝit shal þe   165
help and þe mede turne to þe next of his kyn in
purgatory and hastily spede ham out of har purgatory, ffor þat is a stid of mercy and clensynge
for mannys syn. And nowher els als fast þay shal
haue so grete mercy pat, þroȝ þe myȝt and þe mercy   170
of God and þe   virtue of these holy masses, þay
shalle sone be broȝt out of har peynes and be
ledde to heigh paradise, whar Adam was first, and
þer to be wesshed in the welle of grace with the
watyr of clensynge and to be enoynted with oyl of   175
mercy.

        "Nomore I can tel of þe blesse as ȝit for I
know noȝt ȝit bot peynes. And þerfor what man or
womman þat is of power, mak þay þese holy masses
to be seid for ham, and if þay wer in þe grettest   180
peyne of purgatory, he shold sone be delyuered of
ham and of al oþer, if þese masses be said in the
fourme lyk as I haue told þe, with other good
dedes and almes-doynge, as hit was þe dedys wille.
And if a man or a womman be noȝt in power to make   185
þese masses be ⁺ seid for hym, mak he þese xiij
masses to be seid for hym in þe maner forsaid with
Miserere folwynge and Veni creator. Bot þe masses
of Our Lady shal be Salue sancta parens. And whan
þese masses bene seid, þey shal be sone out of   190
peyne." And fader, al þese I had þe fyrst nyȝt.

        And þan, fadyr, whan sho had seid al þese
wordis, þe lytell hound and þe catte þat broȝt hyr
to me had hyr to hyr peyne agayne. And ȝit ar sho

went fro me, sho seid I shold / se hyr þe next   157v
ny3t in al hyr torment3 ar sho came agayne to me,   196
and how vij deuelles shold torment hyr, and how þe
lytell hounde and þe catte shold euer be with hyr
in fyr to encresce hyr peynes, and how þe worme of
conscience shold euer gnaw hyr with-in. And þat,   200
sho said, was þe grettest peyne þat was in
purgatory or in helle, ffor þat, sho seid, cessed
neuer als lange as euer þay wer in purgatory.

        And þan I asked þe spirite, "What knowest þou
þe peyne of helle, sethen þou cam neuer þer-in?   205
Ffor what can þou telle of ham more than of þe
ioyes of heuyn?"

        And þan sho seid, "3is, by the ryghtwisnesse
of God and by reson, ffor wel I wote þat þe worme
of conscience is most pryve both her and ther.   210
Bot mor can I no3t telle þe of helle, for I haue
no leve, as other haue hadde þat haue appered to
þe or þis. And of hevyn I told þe befor--how þat
when I wer out of purgatory I shold be ledde in-to
erthly paradise and be wesshed [in] þe welle of   215
grace and clensed and be enoynted with oyle of
mercy--and I seid more kouth I no3t telle the of
heuyn for I came no3t 3it therin. And þerfor,"
sho seid, "I tel the som party of helle and som
partie of heuyn." And with that word sho seid   220
farwelle and named my name. "And tak þou now good
hede of my peynes þis ny3t folwynge and also of
other, ffor þou shalt see both myn and other."
And with þat sho 3ede a-way with stronge scryche
and a grete crye. And, as me tho3t, sho seid, "O   225
der lady, be my help." And þan, my der fadyr,
sone aftyr I woke, and by þat tyme [hit] smote one

aftyr mydnyȝt, and whan I began to slep, hit smote
xi.

And on þe morow when I risse vp, I went to   230
Maister Fforest, my gostly fadyr, and told hym
whate he shold do for hyr, and forsoth he graunted
als faste.

I went to Sir John Wynbourne, my oþer gostly
fadyr, and told hym whate he shold do for hyr, and 235
he graunted also, and so did al þe prestes þat sho
spake of þat sholden synge for hyr.

Now fadyr, þe next nyȝt vpon þat folwynge I
went to bed and fel on slepe, and sodeynly was
shewed to me hyr peynes / in purgatory and oþer   158r
many.   And fadyr, neþer sho ne none oþer spirite   241
lad me þerto, bot when I was on slep, me þoȝt I
saw þa[m] als faste without eny ledynge.   And
anone me þoȝt I saw Margaret in hyr wyrst clothes
as she went on erth and in the grettest fyr of þe   245
þe, þe whiche I saw byfore in purgatory.

And me þoȝt I saw about hyr vij deuelles.
And one of ham cloþed hyr with a longe goun and a
longe traille folwynge hyr, and þat was ful   of
sharp hokes with-yn.   And þe goun and þe hokes me   250
þoȝt weren al rede fyr.   And þan þat same deuyll
toke [wormys and pych and tarr and made lokedes
and sett ham vpon hyr hede and he toke] a lange
grete addyr and put al about hyr hede, and þat me
þoȝt hyssed in hyr hede as hit had bene hote   255
brennynge yren in cold watyr.

And me þoȝt sho cried whan sho was so arayed
þat me þoȝt al þe world myȝt haue herd hyr, and þe

lytell hound and þe catte frette in-sondyr hyr
leggis and hyr armes.   260

     And þan seid þat deuyll þat arayed hyr þus,
"This shal þou haue for þi foul stynkynge pryde
and boste þat þou vsed in þe world agayns
mekenesse, and þis hound and þis catte shal euer
frette þe whils þou art her for þyn unresonable   265
loue þat þou loued ham in erth. Ffor I am   þe
deuyll of pride, and þerfor I shal do myn office
in this peyne and quyte þe þy mede for þe seruice
þat þou serued me."

     And me þoȝt many deuelles were with hym. And   270
þan als fast me þoȝt þer came out oþer vj
deuelles, and one pulled out hyr tonge, and anoþer
pulled out hyr hert, and me þoȝt þay raked hit
with iren rakes. "And þis," þay said, "þou shalt
haue for þy wreth and þyn envy, for false   275
forswerynge, for bakbytynge and sklaundrynge--for
al þese þou vsed in þy lyf. And we bene þe
deuelles of wreth and of envy. And al þese addres
and snakes þat þou seest with vs shal turment þe
for þy wikked vices þat þou vsed in erth and did   280
noȝt þi penaunce ar þou came her."

     And þan me þoȝt þer came out oþer two
deuelles, of þe which one hadde sharp rasours, and
he ferd as he wold al to-kyt hyr fleishe, and so
he didde to my syght. /   And me þoȝt he pared   158v
away al hyr lyppis, and he toke a grete hoke of   286
iren and smote þroȝ-out hyr hert, and þat oþer
devill melted lede and brymstone and al maner
stynkynge venym that man myȝt thynk. Also, he
ordeyned to hyr all maner lyknes of mettis and   290
drynkes þat was delycate in this world whiche þat

sho vsed to styr hyr more to syn þan to vertue.
And þose mettys me þoȝt weren al addres and
snakes, and þat þay made hir to ette a-gayne hyr
wille. And þay made hyr to drynke al maner cursed   295
venym and seiden,   "Ette and drynk þis for thy
stynkynge glotony and myspendynge, wastynge and
takynge ouer-mychel while þou was on lyf."   And
þan me thoȝt þese deuelles þat cutted away hyr
fleish and hyr lyppis and threst þe hoke þroȝ hyr   300
hert, þay drew hyr in-to a grete blake watyr, and
þat semed as cold as eny yse, and mychel þer-of
was froren to my syȝt. And þer-in pay kest hyr
and possed hyr vp and doun and seyden, "Take the
this bath for þy sleuth and þi glotony." And þan   305
as fast þay toke hyr out of þe watyr and þrew hyr
in-to a gret fyr, and þer þay lefte hyr stille.
And þat þay seid shold be hyr bed for þe sleuth
þat sho louet so wel her in erth and wold noȝt
come to Goddis seruice when sho myȝht. And þer   310
þay lefte hyr stille with many wormys about hyr.

    And þan me thoȝt þer came oþer two deuelles;
and one broȝt myche .gold and syluer, and þat was
molten and casten in hyr þrote, and þat ran out of
hyr stomake. And he seide, "Take þe þis for þ[i]   315
cursed and wikked coueitise, for þy myspendynge in
wast whan þou had hit and wold noȝt help oþer þat
had nede, and for þy mysgouernaunce when þou had
hit."

    And þan me thoȝt þat oper deuell broȝt hyr to   320
a grete vessel of brasse, and þer-in was al maner
of stynkynge thynge and al maner of venym and
wormys both smale and grete. And in þis grete
vessele þay put hyr amonge þis grete fowl venym

and al to-drow hyr lym fro lym and seid, "Tak þe   325
þis bath for þy vile, stynkynge lechery."

    And sir, fadyr, me thoȝt she cried horribly
and seid, "Euery-body bewar with me and do har
penaunce ar þay dey and leve þe lust of har wiked
synnes," and seid, "These two develles þat   330
turmenteth me her, þay bene þe develles of
coueitise and lechery."

    And so me þoȝt, my der fadyr, sho was longe
turmented in þese / peynes þe mountaunce of half   159r
an hour. And in al þat tyme me þoȝt I saw hyr   335
noȝt, bot I herd hyr horribly crie, and many tymes
me þoȝt she seid, "Der Lady, help me."

    And me þoȝt I stode alonely and beheld hyr
peynes and many a man and wommanys both, both
seculer and relygious, and wedded men and wommen,   340
and sengle men and wommen. And me þoȝt I saw in
peynes and turmentys what syn man or womman vsed
moste in har lyfe and whiche of þe vij synnes þay
loved best, euery man in his degre. Bot amonge al
þo peynes and amonge al Cristen peple, me þoȝt   345
lechery was sorest chastised, and specialy of men
and womm[e]n of Holy Chirch, wheþer þey wer
religiouse other seculer. Me þoȝt, fadyr, þat
prestes and har wommen I saw in peynes, and þay
wer bounden to-giddyr with yren cheynes as for þe   350
most partie. Bot som prestes þer wer þat had
wommen þat wer noȝt bounden to-geddyr as þe oþer
wer, bot þay had ner as myche peynes outward to my
syȝt as þay had, bot noȝt inward.

    Me þoȝt þe peynes of prestes and of har   355
wommen wer þese. Me thoȝt þey wer casten in-to
derk pittis ful of strange fyr, and al maner of

þynge þat myȝt melt to eche har peynes was þrowen
in to ham. And me þoȝt þat pit was full of addres
and snakes and of al wikked wormys, and þer me   360
þoȝt þay wer so turmented þat al þe creatures in
þe world kouth noȝt tel har peynes. And þan me
thoȝt, my der fadyr, þay wer taken out of þe pitte
and casten in-to a strange depe watyr, and þat me
þoȝt was mychell frosen þer-of for þat semed as   365
cold as eny yse. And þer me þoȝt þe devell with
strange hokes al to-drow har fleishe.

   And þan, fadyr, me þoȝt also þer hange ouer
þe watyr many heigh gebbetȝ--as men letteth doun a
boket in-to a welle to draw watyr with-al--and   370
þese gebbetȝ wer ful me þoȝt of / sharp rasours,   159v
and þay wer croket me thoȝt as þay wer hokes. And
me þoȝt þese rasours wer put in the prestes
þrottes and come out at har mowthes. And me thoȝt
þat þay weren plonget vp and doun in þat stynkynge 375
watyr as men wold plonge a boket in-to a welle,
and whan þay wer lange pyned, þan þay wer taken
doun and broȝt out of þat watyr. And sodeynly þay
wer casten in-to stronge fyres. And þese deuelles
keste oyle and greishe to ham and blew fast with   380
stronge belyes þat I myght se no-thynge of ham.
And þan sone aftyr me þoȝt [þese] deuelles leid
ham on anyvelles as smythes done brennynge iren
and smoten on ham with hameres--al þo prestes, bot
noȝt har wommen, ffor þay wer me þoȝt lowsed fro   385
ham. And [þan] me þoȝt þay cried so horribly þat
al þe world myȝt noȝt make so horrible a noyse and
so hiddouse a crie. And þan me þoȝt þat þe
deuelles token brennynge metaille as hit semed
rede gold, and al hote þay put hit in þe prestes   390

mowthes, and þat brennynge ran þrogh-out har
bodies. And þan a deuyl seid, "Take ȝow þis swete
draght for þe fals myspendynge of Goddis goode þat
ȝe spend in wast, in cursed lechery, and about
ȝour false glotony and ȝour wikked pride."   395

Also, fadyr, þese deuelles tok out þe prestes
tonges, and me þoȝt þay kot ham evyn in-sondyr.
And þan me þoȝt þese develles seid, "Tak ȝow þis
peyne in ȝour tonges for ȝour fals and foule
sclaundrynge wordes þat ȝe spake þer-with of   400
lechery and broȝt many womm[e]n to þat syn and out
of   har   goode   lyvynge--both   nunes,   wyfes,
ankeresses, sengle wommen and maydnesse, and many
wommen þat neuer wold haue done þat syn. ȝe with
ȝour fals gold and plesynge speche haue broȝt ham   405
to syn, wher-þrogh þay bene her peyned with ȝow
for þe lust þat þay had þer-of and þe coueitise of
ȝour gold and wold noȝt do penaunce þer ar þay /   160r
deyed; þerfor, þay shal ful der aby hit her."

þan me þoȝt þat þe deuelles hadden many sharp   410
rasours in har handes, and to some of þo prestes
þay pared of har crownes--and hit semed + har
fyngres and har lyppis--and seiden, "Tak ȝow this
for ȝe haue myspendet ham; and also for ȝe hedes
and prelates of Holy Chirche shold haue chastised   415
syn both in ȝourself and in ȝour housholdes and in
ȝour lymys and in ȝour suggetȝ vnder ȝow, and ȝe
did noȝt; and for ȝe suffred so ham for coueitise
of   gold   and   flattrynge   wordis,   þat   þay   myȝt
consent þe soner to ȝour wille what ȝe wold haue   420
done."

And þan me thoȝt þe deuelles tok brennynge
eddres and put þroȝ þe prestes eers and seiden,

Take ȝe this, for ȝe wer prelatȝ of Holy Chirche
and ȝe wold neuer hyr trouth when ȝe didde amysse,   425
bot vttrely destrued ham whan þay told ȝow eny-
thynge agayne ȝour wille."

   And þan me þoȝt þe deuelles toke out har
hertis and in har hertis þer was a stronge worme
and þat frette in-sondre al þe hert-strenges and   430
al membres of har bodies with-in. And þan seid þe
deuelles, "Tak ȝe [þis] worme of conscience þat
neuer shal stynte gnavynge ne frettynge with-in
til ȝour synnys be forgeven, and þat shal be þe
cause ȝe wold noȝt forsake ȝour syn, ne do   435
penaunce þer-for, ar þat ȝe shold be dede. Also,
ful ofte ȝe receyuet ȝour God ful vnworthyly and
handlet hym ful vnhonestly, and þat was for ȝour
stynkynge syn of lechery and al oþer synnys also
agayn ȝour conscience. þerfor bene ȝour crownes   440
and ȝour fyngres pared, and ȝe ben degraded her
for ȝour mysgouernaunce agayne ȝour presthode."

   And þan me thoȝt I saw many deuelles renne
about ham and al to-drow har priue membres both of
þe prestes and of har wommen. Bot me thoȝt þat   445
relygious men and wommen + had an hondred tymes
more peynes þan seculers hadde þat weren seculer
prestes and seculer wommen, for þay wer castyn on
strange whelys and turned about with strange fyr.
And eddres and snakes and deuelles wer euer about   450
ham. And þe deuelles turned þe whelys so fast þat
I myȝt noȝt se ham, bot ful horribly þay cried as
al þe world had cried at onys. And þis peyne,
fadyr, had men and wommen of religionse and
prelatis of Holy Chirche more þan seculer prestes   455
or seculer wommen.

Bot almaner / of prestes wer casten in-to 160v
depe pittis and har wommen with ham.   And ful
horribly þay cried to-giddyr, and har crie was
this: "Wo worth pride, couetise, and lechery, and 460
þe wikked lustes of the world, and wo worth þe
wikked willys þat wold neuer her do penaunce whils
þay lyved in this wreched world.   And þerfor her
we shal ful der abye, and euery Cristen man and
womman be-war by vs and forsak syn and do penaunce 465
in his lyf."   And þus me þoȝt, my der fadyr, I
sawe prestes be punshed in purgatory.

And þan, fadyr, me þoȝt sodeynly I saw þe
peynes of nonnes and of monkes synguler and of al
oþer religious wommen withouten any man with ham 470
in what state þay stod in her.   And fadyr, me þoȝt
þe peynes of ham was ouer strange fyr brennynge,
and þe deuelles wer euer rakynge on ham with
strange hokes as me þynke wommen drawen wolle with
cambes.   And al maner of foule venym þay set on 475
ham, and som toke grete longe addres and serpentȝ
and shotten þroȝ-out har heedes brennynge.   And
som sette on har heedes addres als gerlandes to
streyne vp har forhedes, and þat me þoȝt hissed
vp-on har heedes as hit wer brennynge iren in cold 480
watyr.   And me þoȝt þe deuelles tok out har hertis
and al to-drow ham with crokes.   And þen þe
deuelles seiden to ham, "Take her þese addres þat
rennen þrogh-out ȝour hedes for fals myshirynge
þat ȝe had lust in to hyr more idel wordes to styr 485
ȝow to syn þan to hyr good wordes þat myȝt styr
ȝow to vertu which þat falleth to ȝour ordre.
Also, take þese addres þat bynden vp ȝour forhedes
for þe grete streynynge þat ȝe streyned vp ȝours

in ȝour lyf whar-þroȝ ȝe myȝt þe more be stirred   490
to syn."

    Also, fadyr, me thoȝt þe deuelles kut þe
nunnes lippis in-sondre, and þe deuelles bad ham
take þat for har lykerous kyssynge þat þay kissed
men and made many fal to syn þat wold noȝt ne had   495
[þay] bene. Also, me þoȝt þat þe deuelles kest
veillys of fyr vp-on har hedes and þat came doun
to har brewes, and þan seid þe deuelles, "Take her
þese veillys for þe grete shewynge þat ȝe shewed
ȝour face in ȝour lyf--agayne ȝour ordyr--to styr   500
ȝow to syn and oþer / both.   161r

    Than me þoȝt þe deuelles to[k] out har tonges
and set addres þer-on and todes, and þan seid þe
deuelles, "Take ȝe þis for ȝour fals lechery and
foul wordes and foul contenaunce and bakbytynge   505
and sclaundrynge."

    And þan me thoȝt þe deuelles cam doun and al
to-raf har hertis and al har lymmys. And þan seid
þe deuelles, "Tak ȝow this for ȝour wikked slewth
and ymaginacions and foul contenaunce and for ȝour 510
wiked thoghtys þat ȝe lay in."

    And þan me thoȝt þe deuelles and þay made
such a rorynge þat al þe world myȝt þer-of haue
bene aferd þat had hard þat wakynge, as I didde
slepynge. And þus mych, fadyr, sawe I of þe   515
peynes of religious men and wommen.

    Than, fadyr, sone aftyr me thoȝt I saw [þe]
peynes of wedded men and wommen, and þe peynes of
ham was this: thay wer put in-to grete barraylles
ful of addres and snakes and of al oþer maner of   520
stynkynge thynge. And me thoȝt þe barailles wer
fast closed at both þe endes, and þay wer stopped

þer-in. And þan me thoʒt þe deuelles tok lange
gaddys of iren al brennynge and put þrogh-out þe   525
barailles, and as fast as þay myʒt, þay turned ham
about as men don harneis in barrailles, and þan me
þoʒt þe barailles brake and þer smote out such a
smoke þat [hit] al by-smoked ham þat was about.
And þan me þoʒt þe deuelles tok pich and molt hyt   530
and put in-to har þrottʒ, bot hit ran noʒt
þroʒ-out ham bot abode stille with-in ham. And
þan me þoʒt þe deuelles al to-drew euery bone of
ham from oþer. And þan seid þe deuelles to ham,
"Tak ʒe þis bittir bath þat was in these barailles   535
for ʒour wikked and synful lyggynge in ʒour foul
beddes of lechery and for fals brekynge of ʒour
trouth agayns Goddis wille and wold noʒt kep ʒow
to ʒour wyfes and to ʒour housbandes, as þe law of
God wold. Also, tak ʒow this bittyr piche for þe   540
swete mettis and drynkes þat ʒe vsed in ʒour
glotony to fulfil your lechery. Also, take ʒow
þis bittyr drawynge for ʒour softe beddis and   161v
softe werynge þat ʒe vsed to fulfil / ʒour syn,
and also for þe wikked werkes þat ʒe didde agayne   545
Goddis wil and ʒour conscience." And þus me thoʒt
I saw þe peynes of wedded men and wommen.

   And [as fast, fadyr, aftyr þese I saw þe
peynes of sengle men and wommen and þese me þoʒt
was] þat þay wer putte on spittis and rostet, and
as many addres and snakes and todes, and also   550
mychel foul venym as myʒt swarme about ham, was
set on ham to sowk ham and to gnaw ham. And þan
wer þay taken of þese spittis, and þe deuelles
drew ham þroʒ-out þe fyr with hard sharp hokes,

both sengle men and wommen. And þay al for-drow   555
har hertis and har most pryue membres. Than seid
þe deuelles to ham, "Take ȝe þese peynes for ȝe
disused ȝour-self in þe foul lust of lechery and
in al oþer synnys agayne Goddis will and ȝour owne
conscience, and for ȝe disvsed ȝour-self in þe syn   560
of lechery with-out eny nede, when ȝe myȝt haue
had and taken þe fredom of wedloke, which ȝe had
leve by God to take and þat was free and comyn to
euery man and womman þat wer with-out ordre and
þat was vnder þe law of God to be weddet. And so   565
myȝt ȝe haue done and kept ȝow fro lechery, and
for ȝe wold noȝt do ⁺so and for ȝe despised þe
ordre of wedlake, and for ȝe dredded þat, if ȝe
wer weddet, þat oþer men wold tak ȝour wyfes. And
for þis foule mystrust and foule disvse of ȝour   570
body, tak her [þese] bittyr peynes in purgatory
and þese addres and þese snakes euer to .gnaw on
ȝow til our bandes of syn be wasted away and til
God have shewed on ȝow his mercy. Ffor wit ȝe
welle þis is noȝt helle--þis is an instrument of   575
Goddis ryȝtwisnesse to purge ȝow of ȝour syn in
purgatory.   And for ȝe wold noȝt vse penaunce in
ȝour lyfes and ar ȝe came her."   And þus me þoȝt
þese deuelles sayden to al þese sowles þat wer
ther.   And þus myche, my der fadyr, of þe peynes   580
of sengle men and wommen, and al þese me thoȝt I
saw fro the tyme þat þe spirit of Margaret went
fro me.

      And þan sho seid to me, "Now has þou sene my
bittyr peynes þat I suffred in þese ˌgrete fyres of   585
purgatory." And þan, fadyr, as fast me þoȝt þat
sho come out of þis grete vessele and came to me.

And þan sho seid, "Thou may know by þe deuelles
þat weren my tormentours and by þe tormentis þat
þay did me what syn þat I haue done. And þerfor   590
now þay shal / neuer turment me more. God hit þe   162r
ʒeld and al my helpers þat haue sped me out of my
peynes."

    And þan I asked hyr why sho cried so
pittously, "Swete Lady, be my help," and why sho   595
cried more on Our Lady þan on God Almyghty or on
any oþer seynt. And þan she seid, "ʒis, ffor sho
is hede of al oþer seyntes, except God alone, and
for sho is wel of mercy, I cried on hyr in my
grete woo. And also for I shold þe soner be   600
delyuered þroʒ hyr bone and prayer. And also,
whils I was on lyf, I fasted hyr fast." And þe
spirit said me agayne þer shold neuer none failly
of Our Ladies help þat cometh in-to purgatory þat
hath fasted hir fast byfore.   605

    And þan I asked hyr why sho cried so
deelfully in þat grete vessel þat sho was in and
why I myʒt noʒt see hyr. And þan sho seid, "If
þou had sene my peynes, þou sholdest haue bene so
ford þat þy body shold noʒt wel haue borne þy   610
spirit with-out grete tribulaunce of þy wittis or
els stronge sekenesse, for my peynes wer so
stronge. And þerfor I cried so horribly.

    And þan I asked hyr whi þat flaume of fyr
come out at hyr mouth and why at hyr hert come out   615
so many sparkles of fyr and why hyr hert was so
woundet and why þe lytel hound and þe catte folwed
hyr and what goode didde þe masses hyr and prayers
þat sho bade say for hyr. And þan sho seid, as
touchynge þe flawme of fyr at hyr mouth, hit was   620

for hyr grete othes þat sho vsed in hyr lyf, and
also, as touchynge þe wound at hyr hert and the
sparkynge fyr þer-of, hit was for hir othes weren
mych by Our Lordes hert, and þat was þe cause þat
þe sparkes of fyr came out at hyr hert--and þat   625
was one, sho seid, of þe grettest peyne s þat sho
hadde.   And, as touchynge þe litel hound and þe
catte, þay wer hir mawmettes þe whil sho was on
lyve, and sho sett hyr hert to mych on such foul
wormes.   630

"And þerfor þay shal folow me to encresce my
peynes euer til þe bondes of syn be woren in-
sondyr.   And touchynge þe masses sayinge / and þe 162v
prayers þat wer done for me, þay haue hastied me
þe soner out of my peynes.   Also, hethen-forward I 635
shal neuer be tormented more with deuelles saue
with one, and þat is with my wikked angell, and he
shal brynge me þroȝ þese two fyres of purgatory.
And if þer by any drosse of syn, þer shal I be
clensed, and þis hound and þis catte shal neuer   640
folow me more."

And þan sho seid far-welle and named my name
and seid sho shold neuer trauaill me more in þe
syȝt of peynes bot on oþer nyȝt.   And þan me þoȝt
sho went fro me, bot sho cried noȝt as sho did   645
byfore.   And þan, fadyr, I woke of my slep, and
þan me þoȝt I was ful wery and ful al afrayed.
And fadyr, þus mych on þis nyȝt.

And þan, my der fadyr, me þoȝt sho come to me
þe next nyȝt folwynge.   And fadyr, me þoȝt sho was 650
al blake as eny lede, bot sho had no flawme of fyr
in hyr mouth as sho had byfore, and also, þe wound
of hert was closed, and al þe woundes þat me þoȝt

sho had on hyr body byfore wer closed vp. And þan
me þo3t sho said to me, "Tak þou good hede how I   655
shal now be delyuered of my peynes and turne in-to
þe blisse of paradise."

And þan me þo3t sho went fro me. And as
faste a deuell toke hyr and threw hyr in-to þe
medel fyr. And þer me þo3t he had belyes in his   660
hand, and he blew fast, and me þo3t sho lay and
fried in þe fyr as hit had bene fysshe in hote
oyle. And þan me þo3t he toke hyr vp agayne and
led hyr þroghout al þe mydel fyr. And euer as sho
went, þe blaknesse of hyr body went away as hit   665
had bene þe tal3h of a candel when hit dropeth for
hete. And by þat sho come to þe end of þat grete
fyr, me þo3t sho wax al rede and wel colored as
hit had bene blode-[red] fleishe.

And þan me þo3t sho entred into þe þrid fyr,   670
and þis fyr me þo3t was as cler as eny awmbre. /   163r
And þe deuell bro3t hyr al way þer-in, and euer as
sho 3ode in þat fyr, sho wox euer clerer and
clerer. And me þo3t sho taried no3t in þat fyr,
bot me þo3t sho hyed fast out þer-of, and by sho   675
was at þe end, sho wax wonder white and fayr. And
þan me þo3t sho seid,   "Blessed be God and Our⁺
Lady Mary þat I am here now. And God 3eld þe and
ham both that haue helped me so sone þer-to. And
bot þat if I had .grace of helpe, I shold haue bene   680
punyshed in purgatory 3it iij yer lenger. And if
þat I had no3t appered to the and had help of the,
I shold haue had more stronger peyne þan I hadde."

And sho seid, "þer bene thre purgatories.
þat one is þe grete fyr of purgatory þat þou saw   685
me in fyrst, and þat is euyn-lyke to þe peynes of

helle, save we shal be saved and þay noȝt.   And
þese other two fyres bene accounted an-other."

And þan I asked hyr if al þat deyed shold go
fyrst to þe grette fyr, and sho said, "Nay, Jues   690
and Sarasyns deyen and [oþer] hethen peple, and
þay shal neuer come thar.   þay shal go streȝt to
helle, for þay shal neuer be saved.   And al þo þat
comen in the grete fyr of purgatory shal be saued,
what peynes so-euer þay be in."   695

And þan I seid to hyr, "I menet of al
Criste[n] peple and if al Cristen peple shold go
þeder ar þay went in-to þe oþer two fyres."

And þan sho seid, "Nay, sustyr, God forbede!
Ffor þer goth many a thousand to þe mydel fyr þat   700
come noȝt in-to þe grete fyr.   And þat is al þay
þat haue contricion and haue made satisfaccion and
done penaunce for har synnys.   Ffor," sho seith,
"þe grettest fyr is þe grettest reddur of þe
ryghtwysnesse of God þat is in purgatory.   Ffor,"   705
sho seith, "alle dedely synnes þat men or wommen
haue done in þis world þat þay bene shryven of and
haue noȝt done har penaunce ar þay deyed, þay shal
be punyshed in þis peyne.   And also, many a man
and womman þat wil noȝt leve har synnys / or euyn   163v
sodeynly ar þe deth tak ham, and also, many m[e]n   711
and wommen with many shrewed opynyon.   Ffor þay
wil say, may þay haue thre wordes befor har deth,
þay rek neuer--and þat is a foul, perillous word.
Bot ȝit, God of his mercy graunteth to many these   715
wordes whan þay lyen in har deth-bed, ffor hym is
ful loth to lese þat he der boȝt.   And for
shortynge of his wittis and for peynes of his
sekenesse, he shryveth hym as wel as he can and

putteth hym in Goddis mercy.   Al þis maner of   720
peple shal goo to þis fyr til þe bandes of syn be
wasted in-sondyr, some longer and some shortyr,
and al aftyr [as] þay haue [frendis in erthe to
help and al aftyr as þay haue] done good in erthe
ar þay deyed and aftyr as þay haue suffred   725
sekenesse and tribulacions her.   Ffor," sho said,
"a day of sekenesse her and tribulacion shal stand
for a ʒer [in] purgatory, and þat shal be in þe
grete fyr.   Bot al þat cometh in-to þe grettest
fyr shal come þroʒ þe mydel fyr and so euyn þroʒ   730
þe cler fyr and so passe þe peynes of purgatory."

   And sho seide, "Many shal go þrogh þe mydel
fyr and come noʒt in the grete fyr.   And þo bene
þay þat haue done many venyal synnys and haue noʒt
bene shryven of ham bot generally.   And some wer   735
to bene shryven of specialy befor þay deyed and
many forgeten synnys þat came noʒt to mynd or lyʒt
penaunce or ouer-lytell, or ouer-negligently done
þat was enioynet ham to do, or ouer-lytel
repentaunce, or penaunce ioynet and noʒt fulfilled   740
ar þay deyed: al þis peple shal be clensed and
fulfille har penaunce in þe mydel fyr of purgatory
and so come out and go to þe þrid fyr of
clensynge, as I do now.

   "And many gone to the cler fyr as sone as þay   745
ar dede and come no[þer] in-to þe grete fyr, ne
ʒit in the mydel fyr, bot ryʒt goth to þe cler fyr
and so euyn forth to þe blesse.   And þay bene
innocentʒ and holy men and wommen of religions and
ancrasses and ancras and al holy closed peple and   750
al holy martires and confessours, and all maner of
Cristen men and wommen in the world what syn þat

euer þay haue done if har penaunce be fulfilled ar
þay deyed.   And þroȝh þe mercy of [God] / and þe   164r
gret   trust   in   God   or   in   his   mercy   and   þe   755
contricion þat þay haue for har syn, as fast as
þay bene dede, þay shal come to þis þrid fyr of
mercy and so passe to þe blisse of hevyn with-out
mych peyne or lettynge."

     And þan, fadyr, me þoȝt sho seid,   "I   haue   760
declared   to þe þese bittyr peynes of purgatory,
and I wold declar þe two moo purgatories, bot I
may noȝt lange abide.   Bot þis is þe general
purgatory for al men þat bene Cristen.

     "And   an-oþer   is   by   sekenesse   and   grete   765
tribulacions in þis wor[l]de and aftyr contricion
þat þay hadde and aftyr þe pardon þat þay haue
purchased ham in þe world, whils þay wer out of
dedely syn.   Ffor þay may purchace ham so mychel
pardon in this world þat shal for-do al þe peynes   770
of purgatory and lyghtly brynge ham to þe blisse
of heuyn.   And þis is a-noþer purgatory, and þis
is þe purgatory of mercy.

     "The þrid is purgatory [of grace and þat es,
whare a man or a woman hase maste contenede his   775
synnes   and   moste   vsede   þam,   þare   he   sall   be
puneschede if God will gyfe hym grace and come
noghte in þe generalle paynes of purgatorye.   And
þat es callede þe purgatorye of grace, bot þay
sall hafe full grete paynes till God will gyffe   780
þam mercy.   And many swylke spiryts apperes to men
wakynge   in   this   werld,   and   also   in   purgatorye
bothe, and þay bothe come to men and þay telle
whate may helpe þam, and so þay ere delyuered of
þair paynes.   Also, many apperis slepynge to men   785

and wommen in the werlde, als I did to the, and
telles whate may helpe þam and oþer frendes. And
all this es the purgatorye of grace, so þat I hafe
rehersed vn-to the three purgatoryes.   One   es
purgatorye of rightwisenes: þat es, generalle   790
purgatorye þat þou hafe sene by-fore.   The toþer
es purgatorye of mercy.   And the thirde es the
purgatorye] of grace, as I haue told the.

   "Bot euery man and woman þat may, make þese
masses to be seid for hym and þis psalme <u>Miserere</u>   795
<u>mei</u> <u>deus</u> with þis ympne <u>Veni</u> <u>creator</u> <u>spiritus</u> in
the maner as I haue seid before.   And if he be
noȝt of power to make þese masses to be said for
hym, make he þese xiij masses to be said for hym
with þe prayers folwynge before-saide, and God wil   800
þroȝ his mercy soon delyuer hym out of his peyne.
And if þer be eny preste þat wil say ham for
hymself ar he deyed, þey shal reles his peynes in
purgatory, whan he shal come ther-in as sone as
þay wer seide for hym anone aftyr his deth.   A ful   805
heigh thank and mede shold he haue of God for his
trauaille.   Or if he wold saie hit for any frend
of his, hit wer bettyr of hym þan of any oþer man,
and þe more hastilyer þay shal be delyuered out of
har peynes for his good wille and his trew   810
labour."

   And þan sho seid, "Euery man and womman þat
wer letted or wer in any temptacion which þat is
reherced   byfore, say he þis ympne <u>Veni</u> <u>creator</u>
<u>&c.</u>, and þis temptacion / shal sone a-voide from   164v
hym.   And pan als sone thank he his God and haue   816
he mercy and say he <u>Miserere</u> <u>mei</u> <u>deus</u> with v Auees
gretynge to Our Lady."

And þan sho said, "I haue told the al thynges
as God wil and made an end of purgatory. And take   820
good hede whate þou sees me do now. And if þou
had noȝt gone for me to Southwich on pilgrimage in
wirship of God and Our Lady--ffor I had avowed hit
and I myght noȝt do hit and þou hast done hit for
me--and els I shold ful foule haue bene letted on   825
my passage when I shold ben weyed out of my
peynes, and þat shal þou sone see."

And me thoȝt sone aftre þer came a fayr lady
and a fayr yonge man with hyr as he wer of þe age
of xxty wynter. And he broȝt wheyes in his hand,   830
and he was clad al in white clothes. And me thoȝt
þe lady was clad al in white clothes of gold, and
sterres of gold wer in hyr garment, and a rial
croun sho had on hyr hede of gold and a septyr in
hyr hand, and on þe septre end was a lytel croce.   835
And þan sho spake to þe man in white: "Sone," sho
seid, "take þis womman and let hyr be weyet."

And anone sodeynly sho was in þe weyes. And
as fast þe deuell weyed agayns hyr [and] a grete
lange worme with hym, and twyse sho fel doun to þe   840
deuell, and þe deuell reherced al hyr synnes the
whech sho had bene in peynes fore. And þan seid
þe man in white, "Hyr synnes bene forgeuen hyr for
sho hath done hyr penaunce þerfor, and sho [is]
giffen to þe wel of mercy þat is her present--þe   845
quene of heuyn and of erth, emperice of helle and
purgatory, and þe blessed modyr of God. And sho
is giffen to hyr. Whate can þou say to þis
womman?"

And þan me þoȝt þe deuell toke out a grete   850
worme and seid, "Her is þe worme of conscience þat

ȝit shal trauail hyr / of a thynge þat is behynd: 165r
and þat is, sho made a vow to pilgrymage and
fulfilled hit noȝt."

And þan me þoȝt þat fayr lady seid, "Her is   855
one þat hath done hit for hyr, and my son and I
haue geven þis womman mercy.   And fy on þe,
Sathanasse!   þou and þe worme of conscience shal
neuer der hyr more."

And with þat word me thoȝt sho weighed euyn   860
doun to þe fayr lady.   And me þoȝt þe deuell and
þe worme maden a grete cry, and as fast þay voidet
away.   And þan þat fayr lady toke a white cloth
and wrapped al about hyr and said to hyr, "Come
on, doghtyr, with me, and þou shalt receyue þe oil   865
of mercy, and þy conscience shal be made clene.
And ful grete mede shal þay al haue þat haue
helped þe so sone out of þy peyne.   And when þay
shal come to purgatory, þay shal sone fynde þe
grete mercy of Almyghty God and þe soner be sped   870
out of har peynes for þy sake."

And þan as fast þat fayr lady led hyr ou[er]
a stronge brygge, and at þe end was a white
chapell.   And me þoȝt þer came out mych multitud
of peple þat come agayne with fayr procession and   875
myry sange.   And þan þis fayr lady and þe
procession broȝt hyr to a well, and þer al hyr
body was wesshen.   And sodeynly besyde þe welle
was a white chapele, and þis lady and þe
procession broȝt Margaret þerin.   And anone came   880
in xiij men, and one of ham sange a masse.   And me
þoȝt þe fayr lady offred Margarete to hym, and
sodeynly me þoȝt þer was a croun sette on hyr hede
and a septre in hyr hand.

And þan seid þe man þat sange þe masse,   885
"Doghtyr, take her þe croun of grace and mercy and
þis septre of victory, for þou art passed al þyn
enemyes."   And me þoȝt þe man sange out / þe   165v
masse, and whan þe masse was seid, þay went out of
þe chapell euerych one.   And þe man þat sange þe   890
masse toke Margaret with hym and broght hyr to a
golden   ȝate--and þe procession with ham--and he
said to Margaret, "Doghtyr, go in at þis ȝate and
receyue þe blisse of paradise and of heuyn, þe
which þat is þy kynde heritage and þat Adam was   895
in."

And anone I woke and al þynge was vanshed.
Nomore, fadyr, at þis tyme.   Bot God brynge vs to
his kyngedome.   Amen.

Table of Variants

The first notation in the Table of Variants, LTB 1-195, indicates that all three manuscripts are intact until line 195. Since neither T nor B is complete, each time the number of manuscripts varies, this notation will be changed to show which manuscripts are available. The variants are recorded in the conventional manner: the line number followed by the lemma, a closed bracket, the variant, and the corresponding sigil(s). Two variants for the same lemma are separated by a semicolon.

Recorded as variants are transpositions in word order, additions, omissions, and substitutions. The word preceding the addition serves as the lemma in all cases except when the addition follows a punctuation mark, in which case the lemma will be the word following the addition. Substitutions of the definite article for a demonstrative pronoun (or vice versa) are frequent and unrecorded. I record the variant spellings of the priests' names, but otherwise, no purely orthographical or inflectional variants are given. Since there is considerable variation in L, T, and B in the titles <u>Miserere mei deus</u> and <u>Veni creator spiritus</u>, I print L's title and do not record the varying titles of T and B. In T the omissions and repetitions caused by mishandling of the catchwords are not recorded as variants (see explanatory note 18).

The variant closest to the reading of L, or the chosen reading, is given first. When no one variant is appreciably closer to the text's reading, the order is LTB. When the variants correspond, the order is likewise LTB, and only the form of the first manuscript appears. The same editorial practices applied to L (respecting spelling, punctuation, capitalization, and the expansion of contractions and suspensions) are applied to the variants from T and B recorded in the apparatus.

LTB 1-195

1 maner] manere of T.   to] to the   T.
2 al only] only and to Our Lady B; allonely and to
      Oure Lady Saynte Marie   T.
3 non] none othir T.   ne] nothyr B.
4 Der] Wherfor B.   al] om B; and all oyer trew
      Cristyn ffrendis T.   þis] this lytyll B.
      tretis] tretis delygently B.
5 and hireth] to hyre B.
6 with] of B.   how] how yat T; how aftyrwarde B.
7 fadyr] ffadir and said one this wyse T; fadyr als
      thus as folwyth B.
8 My...witte] Ffadir I do 3ow to wiete T; To yow be
      hit knowyn B.
10 Lord] Lorde God B.
11 viij] vij B.
12 fadyr] furthermor B; so T.
13 saw] saue I sawe B.
14-15 whiche...before] ther-of B.
14 to] om T.
15 by] be my confessyone and T.   tellynge] talkyng
      B.
16 Bot] Bod dere T.   I] hit B.   such] om TB.
18 fadyr] dere ffadir T.
19 fadyr] dere ffadir T.   yuel] sore B.   for] of
      B.
21 was] was noghte T; was not B.
24 me þo3t] as semyd me B.   þat euery] eche B; ylk
      a T.
25 sir] om B.
26 euery-on eched] ylkane was eked T; every fyre was
      knytte B.   oþer] otheres ende B.   þre] om B.
27 and (1)] om B.
28 al] alle was in the myddis T.   þat] the B.   and]
      and so T.
29 in] of B.
30 no3t] neuer TB; om L.   þer] ther-in B.
31 pych] om B.   tarr, lede and brynstone] tarre,
      ledde and bromestane and T; brymstone, terre,
      lede, and B.
32 of] om B.   maner (2)] manere of T.
33 and] and of B.   maner] manere of TB.
34 þat] yat hade T.
35 what] that B.   degre] degre that B.
36-37 þat...tho3t] T adds yat; fryst I sawe that B.
37 had] om B.
38 lecherous] lechours T.
39 religious men and wommen] men or women religious
      B.

40 and] or B.
41 sy3t] syghte yat TB.   grete] om B.
43 before] om TB.   whiche] whilke woman T.
44 religious] relygyone T.
44-45 womman whils sho lyved] woman ye while scho
      lyffede T; in hyr lyf B.
45-46 whiche...so] and in that fire scho hade B.
47 at] ther-in B.
48 a dredeful feerdnes] a dredfull fere T; that
      derefull frere B.
48-49 by þat tyme hit] by tyme T; befor that tyme B.
50 ferdnesse] fere B; for fere T.
52 by] by that tyme B.
53 out] owte ye T; to B.   slep] sclepe that B.
54 bot] ande tho I B.   bade] made T.
55 xj] elleuen of ye clokke T.   by] by the tyme that
      B.
57 as fast] than anone B; onone me thoghte T.   me
      tho3t] om TB.
59 and] and as B.
60 woundes] Three minims in L.
61 rent] to-rent B.
62 an] and B.
63-64 þer...an] ther came sparkis ovt of fire and also
out of hyr movth come a B; owte of yat wonde come T.
66 bot] bot if T.
67 by] by the tyme that B.   þe] yat TB.
68 ferd] afferde that B.
69 Jesus Passion] the Passion of Jesus B.
70 þen] om B.
71 stert] streke B.
73 grisly sy3t] gryslynes B.   affrayed] afferdede
      T; aferde B.
75 of] one T; om B.
78 sore trauaillest] fortrayvaylist B.
79 Faderes name and] name of the Fadyr, of B.   and
      (2)] and of B.
80 in] and TB.
84 and] and to TB.
85 And] And yan T.
87 drech] dretthe B.
88 suffre] suffir this B.
89 syn] synnys fforsothe B.
90 þat] the whilke TB.   was] was a B.   a susters]
      soche an B.   religiouse] relegyon T.
91 knowest þat] knowyth well that B; knewe wele and
      also you knewe me when T.
93 And] And than T.   asked] axid of B.
96 þe which] that B.   was and] om T.

97   confessour] gostly fadyr B.   hym] hym to B.
98   he shal] let hym B.
99   <u>Miserere</u>] <u>Misererere</u> L.
100-01 say he...<u>mei</u>] <u>om</u> B.   and þan] <u>om</u> TB.
102 hert and eyghen] <u>his</u> eyne and his hert B.
103 more] more soner B.   relecet] releuyd B.
104 be] <u>After</u> paynes <u>in</u> T.   my] B; hyr LT.   þe]
     the more B.
105 vers] s <u>has the hook that elsewhere indicates</u> er
     <u>in</u> L.
105-06 let...And] onto the ende B.
106 hym] hym to B.
107 <u>creator</u>] <u>creator spiritus</u> to the ende TB.
108 Also] And B.   Sir John] <u>om</u> B.
109 and] and th psalme B.
110 þis] the B.
111 þe] the same B.
113 iij] twa T.
114 and v dayes] and also v days to say B; and saye
     fyve dayes for me T.
116 afor-seid] a-bown-sayde T; as hit is abowyn-saide
     B.   hym] hir T; than B.   warne] <u>om</u> B.   Don]
     Syr B.   Petrus] Perse T; Piris B; Ydorus L.
117 Combe] Cowme T; Chanon B.
118-19 in maner aforsaid] for me in ye manere
     a-bowne-sayde T; <u>om</u> B.
121 And] And also B; <u>Also</u> T.   Bone] Bowne T;
     Romsey B.   say] saye for me T.   two] three T.
122 <u>Salue sancta parens</u>] <u>om</u> TB.
123-24 as hit is aboue-said] als it es abown-sayde T;
     and so forthe B.
125 And] Also TB.   bidde] bid than B.   Don] Syr
     B.   Pery] Perey T; Parrey B.   say] say for me
     T.
126 Seyntes] Sayntes with yis office T.   <u>Gaudeamus</u>]
     <u>Gaudiamus omnes in domino &c.</u> TB.   memories]
     comemoracionis B.
128 aforseid] a-bown-sayde TB.
129-30 þis, to aske þese] to aske yis T; this B.
130 masses] massis and B.   in] on T.
131 said] saide that B.   þat] <u>om</u> B.
132 And] And also B.   asked] axid hyr B.
134 Almyghty God] God Almyghty B.
135 þat] this B.   þis] the B.
135-36 <u>Veni creator</u>] afore-saide T; <u>om</u> B.
136-37 sho shold] sall scho T.
137 þat] the B.
139 aboue-seid] as hit is saide to-forne B.   yf] and
     if T.

140 or (1)] othyr in B.
141 haue] <u>Precedes phrase</u> þrogh þe mercy of God <u>in</u> B.
     knowlech] knaweyng T.
142 this] his TB.   þrogh] thoght B.
143 of þat] from B.   Also] And also T.   if] if a
     TB.   or] or a T.
145 in] in thes B.   thefte] robory B.
146 or] or in T.   any] enny othyr B.
148 al out] <u>Before</u> Veni <u>in</u> TB.   þe] and yase T.
149 hym] ham B.
150 be voidet] be avoydide T; awoyde B.   at] for
     B.
151 I] And I B; And yan I T.   to (1)] for T.   a]
     <u>om</u> B.
153 and] and than B.
154 ther] yat yare TB.   of] <u>om</u> T.
155 for (2)] <u>om</u> TB.
156 as ffor] als for T; than for B; for L.   for a
     soule] <u>om</u> B.
157 C] C massis B.   and (2)] <u>om</u> B.
158 C] halfe an hundreth T.   half an] an B; thre
     T.
159 to (2)] till T; at B.
161 þer] here B.   of] <u>om</u> B.
162 in] of B.   þat ne] but B.
163-64 from...sake] ther-by B.
163 and many] <u>Repeated in</u> L.
164 Bot] And B.
165 3it] yet hit B.
166 mede] remedy B.
167 hastily] <u>om</u> B.   ham] hym <u>canceled and</u> yam
     <u>written above in</u> T; hym B.   of har purgatory]
     ther-of B.
168 þat] purgatorie B.
169 els als fast] ells and anone T; anone B.
171 þe] the grete B.   þay] yat yay T.
173 to] into B.   heigh] erthely T; glorious B.
     first] fyrst made B.
174-75 with...enoynted] <u>om</u> B.
175 with] with ye TB.
177 I can] can I B.   tel] telle the T.
177-78 for I know no3t 3it bot] whyllis I am in B; ne
     <u>before</u> knawe <u>in</u> T.
178 what] what maner B.
179 that is] beyng B.   mak þay] make he T; and
     makyng B.
180 ham] hym TB.   þay] he TB.
181-82 he...oþer] <u>om</u> B.
182 if] and B.   the] <u>om</u> B.

183 told] tolde to B.   with] wyche B.
184 and...dedys] om B.
185 a (2)] om B.   in] of B.   make] make alle T.
186 þese] this holy B.   masses] messis to TB.   be]
     be for L.   he] me B.
187 masses] om T.   forsaid] als I hafe saide vn-to
     the T; as I haue seide vnto the ende B.
188 Bot] And B.
189 Lady] Lady Seint Mary B.
190 be sone] sone be T; sone be delyverid B.   of]
     of yaire T.
191 had] saue B.
192 al] at B.
193 hound] om T.
194 to] om B.   had] lede B.   hyr (2)] om B.
195 þe next] to B.
LT 195-303
203 purgatory] payne T.
209 by reson] by ye reson of ye saule T.   ffor] om
     T.   þat] om T.
210 is] es ye T.   pryve] payne T.
211 þe] om T.
213 þis] this tyme T.
215 in] T; with L.
216 with] with ye T.
221 now] om T.
222 þis] yis nexte T.
224 with] with a T.
227 hit] it T; om L.
233 als faste] anone and yan T.
234 Wynbourne] Wynburne T.
239 and (2)] and so T.
241 many] many one T.   And] Bot T.
242 bot] bot fadir T.
243 þan als faste] yam onone T.
245-46 þe þre] thir T.
249 þat] it T.
252-53 wormys...toke] wormes and pykk and tarre and
     made lokedes and sett yam appon hir hede and he
     toke T; om L.
253-54 lange grete] grete longe T.
255 in] in ye T.
258 þat] als T.   þoȝt] thoghte yat T.
259 frette] forfrette T.
265 frette] frete appon the T.
267 þerfor] yare T.
270 hym] hir T.
271 als fast] onone T.   þoȝt] thoghte yat T.   vj]
     seuen T.

275 for (2)] and for   T.
276 for (1)] and for   T.
279 vs] vs yat   T.
282 þo3t] thoghte yat   T.
284 al to-kyt] forcute   T.
288 maner] manere of   T.
289 Also] And also   T.
290 to] om   T.   maner] manere of   T.
291 world] werlde ye   T.
294 þat] yose   T.
295 And] And also   T.   to] for to   T.   maner] maner
     of   T.
296-97 thy stynkynge] this cursede   T.
298 mychel] mekyll the   T.
299 þese deuelles þat cutted] this deuele and yat oyer
     deuele cutt   T.
300 þro3] in-to   T.
301 þay] and than yay   T.
LTB 303-25
304 the] þou   B.
305 þi] om   B.   þan] om   T.
306 as fast] anone   TB.   hyr] hyr vp   B.   and] and
     anon   B.
309 her in erthe] in errthe here   B.
311 stille] styll and ther scho saate   B.   many] om
     B.
312 tho3t] thoght that   B.
314 in] into   B.
315 he] to hyr they   B.   þe] thow   B.   þi] TB; þe
     L.
316 cursed and wikked] om   B.   for] and for   TB.
320 þat] that an   B.
321 grete vessel] grete ffatte   T; faate   B.
323 smale and grete] grete and smale   B.
324 vessele] fatte   TB.   grete] om   TB.
LB 325-412
325 and] that   B.   lym (2)] othyr   B.   þe] om   B.
326 þis] this for this is thy   B.   vile] foule   B.
327 sir] also   B.
328 with] by   B.   har] his   B.
329 þay] he   B.   dey] dye that is commandid hym by
     his gostly fadyr   B.   leve] forsake   B.   har]
     this   B.
330 and (2)] and also scho   B.
332 and] and of   B.
333 me] I   B.   sho] that scho   B.   longe] om   B.
336 I] om   B.   horribly] om   B.   tymes] a tyme   B.
338 I stode alonely and] alle only I   B.   hyr] all
     tho   B.

339 both (1)] om B.
340 and (2)] also B.
341 and (1)...And] om B.
342 and] and in B.   what] for what maner B.   man
     or womman] the B.
343 moste] most her B.   vij] vij deedly B.
344 man] man and woman B.   his] her B.
345 and amonge] of B.
346 sorest] hardyst and most sorrist B.   of] in B.
347 wommen] women B; womman L.
348 Me] And also me B.   fadyr] om B.
349 in] om B.
351 most] more B.
352 þe] om B.
353 bot] but yet B.   had ner] nygh B.
355 Me] Also me B.   of (2)] om B.
356 þese...wer] om B.
357 derk] depe B.
358 to eche] and eche of B.
362-63 me...fadyr] dere fadyr me thoght that B.
365 was] was so B.   þer-of for þat] that hit B.
     as] also B.
366 þer] om B.
367 to-drow] to threwe B.
368 fadyr] syr B.   ouer] o followed by two minims in
     B.
369 many] many a strong B.
370 draw] drawe vp B.   and] and to my thynkyng B.
371 me þo3t] om B.
372 me tho3t] om B.   þay] hit B.
373 in] throghe B.
374 at] of at B.
374-75 me tho3t þat] semyng to me B.
376 wold] om B.   in-to] in B.
377 lange...wer] om B.
378 And] then B.
379 stronge fyres] a strong fire B.
380 keste] cast in B.   greishe] pycthe B.
382 þan] om B.   þese] the B; þay L.
383 on anyvelles] vpon stithis B.
384 on] om B.
384-86 bot...ham] om B.
386 þan] then B; þat L.
388 þat] om B.
389 hit] me B.
390 þay] om B.   in] into B.
391 and þat brennynge ran] and than that ren brennyng
     B.
392 3ow] ye B.

393 þe] <u>om</u> B.
394 in (2)] and in B.
395 3our false] fulle and stynkyng B.
396 fadyr] sir, semyng to me that B.
397 me þo3t þay] <u>om</u> B.
398 þan] also B.   þo3t] thoght that B.   3ow] ye
     B.
401 wommen] womman L; a woman B.   þat] <u>om</u> B.
402 of] <u>om</u> B.
403 sengle] gentyl B.
404 syn] synne that B.
405 haue] <u>om</u> B.
406 her] <u>om</u> B.
407 þe (1)] the full B.
408 þer] <u>om</u> B.
410 þan] And also syr B.   þat] <u>om</u> B.
412 þay] <u>om</u> B.   semed] semed and L; semyd to me
     also B.
L 412-515
432 þis] þese L.
446 wommen] wommen þat L.
496 þay] 3e L.
502 tok] to L.
LT 515-899
515 sawe I] I sawe T.
516 men and] <u>om</u> T.
517 Than, fadyr] And than T.   þe] T; <u>om</u> L.
519 was this] were thiese T.   in-to] in T.
520 oþer] <u>om</u> T.
522 fast] anone yan T.
528 hit] it T; <u>om</u> L.
530 in-to] in T.   bot] bot ffadir T.
532 euery] yam ylke a T.
534 3e] 3ow T.
536 and] and also T.
545 tho3t] thoghte, dere ffadir T.
547-49 as...was] onone fadir after thiese I sawe ye
     paynes of synglere men and wymmen and yase me
     thoghte was T; þan me þo3t L.
550 todes] tades and newtes T.
554 fyr] fyres T.
556 Than] and yan T.
557 3e (1)] 3owe T.
562 had and] <u>om</u> T.
563 take] take to T.
564 euery] euerylke a T.
565-66 my3t 3e] also 3e myghte T.
567 do] <u>Repeated in</u> L.
569 wold] wolde hafe T.

570   and] and ye T.
571   þese] thiese T; þis L.
575   þis] bot this T.
576   ry3twisnesse] ryghtewysnes and T.
579   to al þese sowles] om T.
580   der] om T.   fadyr] fadir I saw T.
583   me] me til scho come a-gayne and sone after scho
      come agayne to me T.
586   as fast me þo3t] me thoghte onone T.
587   vessele] fatte T.
591   now] om T.
592   3eld] for3elde T.
596   þan] yan scho did T.
600   soner] rathere T.
601   also] also the T.
607   vessel] fatte T.
615   at (1)] of T.
616   sparkles] sparkes T.
618   þe] yase T.   and prayers] and yase prayers hir
      T.
620   hit] þat T.
622   as] om T.
626   peynes] paynnes T; peyne L.
631   þerfor] yare T.   shal] om T.
632   euer] ay T.
635   soner] tytter T.   Also] And also fro T.
640   and (2)] ne T.
647   al afrayed] euylle afferde T.
648   mych] mekill me thoghte I sawe T.   þis] yat T.
650   And] And yan dere T.
651   lede] cole T.   of fyr] After mouth in T.
653   of] at hir T.
656   turne] enter T.
658-59 as faste] onone T.
665   body went] felle T.
666   þe] om T.
669   blode-red] blode-rede T; blode and L.
671   þis] that T.
673   in] þer-in T.
675   þer-of] yar-of till scho was at the ende T.   by]
      by ye tym T.
677   and Our] Repeated in L.
679   both] all T.   me] om T.
680   þat if] if yat T.   had] had hafed T.
682   had (2)] had hade T.
684   And] And than T.   thre] thre manere of T.
685   þat] om T.
687   þay] yay sall T.
690   fyrst] om T.   þe] ye fyrst fyre yat was to yat

```
       T.
691   oþer] T; out  L.
692   þay] Bot yay  T.    go] om  T.    to] to ye paynes
      of  T.
693   þo] om  T.
695   so-euer] yat euer  T.
696-97 of...and] om  T.
697   Cristen] Cristel  L.
698   in-to] to  T.
699   forbede] forbede it  T.
701   no3t] om  T.    in-to] in  T.    þay þat] lesse or
      mare thurgh grace als yay  T.
709   þis payne] ye paynnes of purgatorye  T.
711   ar þe deth] yat dede  T.
711-12 men and wommen] man and wommen  L; a man and
      woman  T.
712   with many] hase many a  T.
713   deth] dede  T.
715   his] his heghe  T.    to] om  T.
716   deth-bed] beddis of ded  T.
722   longer] langer tym  T.
723   as] als  T; om  L.
723-24 frendis...haue] frendis in erthe to helpe and
      all after as yay hafe  T; om  L.
725   as] yat  T.
726   her] here in yis erthe pacyently or yay dyed  T.
727   her] After tribulacyone in T.
728   in] Four minims in L.
734   þat haue done] yat hase done repeated in T.
735   of] of in  T.
737   ly3t] oure-lyghte  T.
746   noþer] T; no  L.    in-to] in  T.
748   euyn forth] onone  T.    þay] yat  T.
750   ancrasses and ancras] ancres and ancresys  T.
751   and (1)] And God hym-selfe schewede his blyssede
      modyre to see ye paynes of purgatorye yose yay
      neghede hir noghte  T.
754   þrogh] om  T.    God] T; om  L.
756   as fast] anone  T.
760   þrogh] om  T.    God] T; om  L.
762   declar] declare to  T.
765   And] om  T.
766   worlde] 1 omitted in L.    aftyr] after ye  T.
768   whils] ye while  T.
771   þe] om  T.
772-73 and þis is þe purgatory] om  T.
774   is] After purgatory in T.
774-93 of...purgatorye] T; om  L.
794   euery] euerylke  T.    and] or  T.
```

797   if] <u>om</u> T.
798   masses] messes alle T.
799   masses to] <u>om</u> T.
801   hym] yam T.   his] yaire T.
804   as (1)] also T.
805   A] And a T.
807   if] <u>om</u> T.
812   Euery] Euer ylk T.
813   letted or] lettirde yat T.   is] I <u>supralinear in</u>
      T.
815   þis] ye deuele and yat T.
816   þan als sone] anone yan T.
816-17 haue he] aske his T.
817   he (2)] <u>om</u> T.
819   I haue] Now hafe I T.
820   And] And now T.
822   for me] <u>After</u> pilgremage <u>in</u> T.   in] in ye T.
823   and] and of T.
824   I] <u>om</u> T.
825   on] of T.
826   shold] solde hafe T.   my] yise T.
828   aftre] aftyr yat T.
829   as he wer] <u>om</u> T.
832   al] <u>om</u> T.   clothes] clothe T.
835   septre end] ende of the septre T.
839   as fast] onone T.   hyr] hir and T.
841   the] <u>om</u> T.
844   hyr] <u>om</u> T.   is] es T; <u>om</u> L.
845   her] <u>om</u> T.
846   and (2)] and of T.
850   a] yat T.
852   of] for T.
853   to] to a T.
855   þat] that yat T.
858   Sathanasse] foule Sathanas T.
862   as fast] anone T.
864   and (2)] and yan this lady T.   to hyr] <u>om</u> T.
872   as fast þat] onone this T.   ouer] oure T; o
      <u>followed by two minims in</u> L.
873   þe] ye brygges T.   a] a faire T.
875   agayne] agaynes hir T.
877   a] a fayre T.
890   euerych one] ylkane T.
892   ham] hym T.
894   þe (2)] <u>om</u> T.
897   anone] anone ffadir T.

Explanatory and Textual Notes

See the Works Consulted for full citations of the sources identified parenthetically in the notes below.

7   "gostly fadyr": 'a father confessor' [OED Ghostly 1.c.].

8   "do...to witte": 'make known to, inform' [OED Do B.III.22.c.].

9-10   Saint Lawrence's Day is August 10. In The Pylgremage of the Sowle, Guillaume de Deguileville's "merueylous dreme" likewise occurs on "Saynt Laurence nyght" (fol. 2r).

10   B has the date "1422" in the right margin at fol. 10r.20.

13-15   At 19-20 and 212 are further allusions to the visionary's previous experiences.

16   The accompaniment of a guide is a convention in the otherworld journeys. Often in the course of the journey, usually at a critical point, the guide disappears, leaving the visionary precariously alone (Os 25-26). The announcement here at the outset is perhaps intended to heighten our anticipation. At 20-21 and 218-21 we are again reminded of the visionary's isolation.

18   T ends fol. 250v with "so" and the bracketed "danly" as a catchword, yet fol. 251r begins "sodanely." Although at fol. 253r.19 in T the scribe writes "so sodaynely," where L lacks "so" (xxx), the reading at fols. 250v-251r apparently results from the mishandling of the catchword. At fols. 254r-254v, 254v-255r, and 255v-256r in T, there is confusion of the catchwords, causing omissions and repetitions in T; these errors are not recorded as variants in the apparatus.

24   The fires may have been suggested by the four fires of falsehood, covetousness, discord, and iniquity in the Vision of Furseus, which Bede recounts in the Historia ecclesiastica 3.19 (273). The vita of Saint

Lawrence in the <u>Legenda aurea</u> offers another possible
source: "Saint Lawrence had three inward fires,
whereby he conquered the lesser fires without. The
first was the greatness of his faith, the second his
burning love, the third his true knowledge of God,
which penetrated him like a fire" (Jacobus de Voragine
445).

26   "eched": 'expanded, grew' [<u>MED</u> <u>eken</u> 4.(a)].
The verb was apparently unfamiliar to the B scribe.
Here he substitutes "knytte"; at 358, where the
infinitive "eche" occurs, meaning `increase'[<u>MED</u> <u>eken</u>
1.(a)], he misconstrues the verb as the pronoun <u>each</u>.

30   "noȝt": For a discussion of this emendation,
see p. 54 above.

39-40   "Religious" men and women are those bound by
monastic vows or to a religious order; "seculers" are
unconfined. Men and women "of ordyr" is the inclusive
phrase, meaning all those in the ministry of the
Church.

44   The similarity of a small B-shaped <u>s</u> to a
broken-circle <u>e</u> and the ambiguity of two minims make
the words <u>religious</u> and <u>religione</u> easily confused.
That the adjective can be used substantively adds to
the potential confusion. Although the variant reading
in T "house of relygyone" is well supported [<u>OED</u>
<u>Religion</u> 1.c. 'House...<u>of religion</u>, a religious house,
a monastery or nunnery'], the reading in L "house of
religious" is retained here and at 83 (where T again
reads "relegyon" for L's "religiouse"). In L
"religious" is a plural substantive, supported by <u>OED</u>
<u>Religious</u> B.1. See 414 and 688 where the plural
substantive is "religions(e)." At 40 and 83 B is not
recorded as a variant. In both instances the word ends
ambiguously in two minims over which is a circumflex;
this identical ending at 36 in B is expanded
"religiou<u>s</u>," where an adjective is demanded.

51   "a lytel mayd child with me": See the
remarks on pp. 26 and 37-38 above.

52   "þe vij psallmes": the Penitential Psalms
(numbers 6, 32, 38, 51, 102, 130, and 143).

52   "þe lytany":   'an appointed form of public
prayer, usually of a penitential character' [OED
litany].

52-53   In the Gast of Gy after the wife and clerks
say the "seuen spalmes [sic] with þe letany"--then
three times the "agnus dei"--the spirit's voice is
heard (Yorkshire 2:296, lines 226-27).

70-72   In the afterlife visions, the visionary is
often menaced by devils. For example, devils threaten
Drythelm with burning tongs, though they do not
actually seize him (Bede 493). The participation of
the visionary in the punishments reaches an extreme in
the Vision of Tundale; among his numerous torments is
his consumption by the beast Acheron, wherein "he is
tortured by dogs, bears, lions, serpents and many other
creatures, as well as by more demons, violent fire and
cold, and by his own burning tears and gnashing teeth"
(D. D. R. Owen 29). The threat in the Revelation ("she
wold haue cast fyr on me") recalls most directly the
experience of Furseus: "...the evil spirits seized one
of those who were burning in the flames, hurled him at
Fursa, hitting him and scorching his shoulder and jaw"
(Bede 273-75). While the motivation in Furseus is
clear (the soul thrown at Furseus was that of a usurer
from whom Furseus had accepted a garment), in the
Revelation there is no apparent reason why the spirit
of Margaret should threaten the visionary.

77-84   In the Gast of Gy, the prior likewise
"coniore[s]" the spirit, asking him, "whether ertou ane
ill gaste or a gude?" (Yorkshire 2:297, line 257).

93   In the right margin of L (fol. 156r.14) is
the phrase "Nota missas." In the left margin of T
(fol. 251v.19) is a cross, followed by "here askedᵉ
sche helpe in þe name of God." B has "Nota xiijᵉ
Misse" in the right margin at fol. 11r.5.

97   "my confessour": referred to as "Maister
Fforest" at line 209-10. See pp. 33-35 above for the
historical identification.

99   "Miserere mei deus": Psalm 51 (50 in the
Vulgate), one of the Penitential Psalms. The Miserere
and Veni creator spiritus follow the Revelation in the
Thornton Manuscript (fol. 258r).

108   "Sir John":   referred to as "Sir John Wynbourne" at line 212.   See pp. 35-37 above for the historical identification.

112-13   "þe recluse of Westmyster":   See pp. 30-32 above for the historical background.

116-17   "Don [Petrus] Combe":   For historical identification, see the discussion on p. 32 above.   I emend "Ydorus" with "Petrus" as opposed to "Piers" on the assumption that the L scribe misinterpreted initial p as y, the broken-circle e as a looped d, and t as o.

121, 125 "Sir Richard Bone" and "Don John Pery": For historical identification, see p. 35 above.

133   In the right margin of T (fol. 252r.13) is the note: "þe virtue of þis spalme [sic] Miserere mei deus."

141   In the left margin of L (fol. 156v.21) is the note: "Nota virtutem psalmi Miserere and Veni creator."

147   In the right margin of T (fol. 252r.24) is the note: "þe virtu of þis ympne vni [sic] creator spc qui paraclitus diceris &c."

154   In the left margin of B (fol. 11v.12) is the note: "Nota CCC Massis."   This is a curious note, since B, like L, prescribes 350 masses; T alone totals 300.

156-59 Despite the spirit's agreement that the masses of Our Lady, St. Peter, and the Trinity are more profitable than the Requiem mass, her recommendation is for one hundred of Our Lady, the Trinity, and Requiem, and fifty of St. Peter. T's variant (fifty of Requiem) does not remedy the inconsistency, though it is identical to the prescription that Gy's spirit submits to the prior (Yorkshire 2:330, lines 1944-50).

159   "to" (1): 'in addition to' [OED To, prep. A.V.15.].   Given the word "folwynge" at line 170, `after' would be apt.

164-69 This assurance that prayers said for a damned soul would be transferred to his next of kin in purgatory is perhaps intended to dispel the common "fear to pray, sing psalms or say masses for...[an] unrepenting sinner"--a fear that was "in accordance with the doctrines of the Church" (Os 34). Also, "the fact that the saying of masses for the dead formed a considerable part of the revenue of the clergy" (Os 32) may have prompted the introduction of this economical notion of the prayers.

173   "heigh paradise, whar Adam was first": the earthly paradise (cf. 894-96). Here T reads "erthely" paradise, which is L's reading at 215.

174   "welle of grace": Within the earthly paradise in the Vision of Tundale "was a welle/The feyryst that any mon myght of telle"--"the well of lyfe" (lines 1557-58, 1559). Cf. the New Testament Rev. 7.17. Also see the note at 599 below on the reference to Mary as the "wel of mercy."

179-90   The third-person plural pronouns þay and ham in lines 179 and 180; the reversion to the singular he at 181, 186, and 187; and the return to the plural at 190 demonstrate the confusion arising from a singular antecedent of indefinite gender.

187   In the left margin of T (fol. 252v.18) is the note: "qualiter xiij messis debent dici."

194   "had hyr to hyr peyne": 'led her to her pain' [MED haven 8. and OED Have B.I.16.].

199-200 "þe worme of conscience": Bernstein has drawn attention to Augustine's discussion of hellfire in the City of God, a discussion based "upon Isaiah 66.24, 'their worm shall not die, their fire shall not be quenched.'" Augustine "prefers the idea that both the fire and the worm apply to the body" and seemingly "concludes...that these corporeal pains in turn inspire subjective, internal suffering in the soul." Bernstein cites "Peter the Chanter (d.1197) [who] echoes the City of God 21.9 as he affirms that `the evil person in hell is tormented, even for venial sins, in a double way, that is, both by material punishment and by the worm of conscience'" (518-19, 523). In Guillaume de Deguileville's Pylgremage of the Sowle, a work translated into Middle English prose in 1403, the worm of conscience, or Synderesys, is called forth by Satan to bear witness against the pilgrim's soul. Chaucer's

Physician refers to the worm of conscience at line 280 in his closing exhortation (Robinson 147).

204-07   The   visionary's   question   echoes   Gy's admission that he knows nothing of hell since he was "neuer þare ne never sal be" and will not enter heaven until "clene of sin" (Yorkshire 2:301, lines 468-70).

210   "most   pryve":   'most   private,   inward.' Clearly, a scribe might easily confuse "pryue" and "peyne." L's reading ("pryve") is retained, since the reading in T ("payne") is an easier reading, especially given   the   phrase   at   201,   "þe   grettest   peyne." Chaucer's Physician, it may be noted, uses the adjective in his closing exhortation, line 281:   "no man woot...in which manere wyse/The worm of conscience may agryse/Of wikked lyf, though it so pryvee be/That no man woot therof but God and he" (Robinson 147).

215   The emendation "in" for "with" is supported by the reading of T as well as by the phrase at 174 "in the welle."   The reading "with" may represent the anticipation of the phrase "with oyle of mercy" (216-17).

225-26   Whether the spirit's cry is addressed to the visionary or to Mary is unclear. Here it seems to be directed to the dreamer. (See 65-66 and 91-92 where the spirit demands the dreamer's help and 681-83 where she thanks the visionary.) At 337 we may assume the cry is directed to Mary, since the visionary has discharged Margaret's requests; the exchange at 594-605 also implies that Mary is the one intended.

227-29   I.e., the vision recounted in lines 57-226 occurred between eleven and one o'clock.

252-53   The emendation corrects the homoeoteleuton in L.

252   "lokedes":   'lovelocks,   curls'   [MED   loket n.(1)].

263   "agayns":   'instead of'   [OED Against, prep. V.14.].

271   "vj deuelles":   Horstman emends T's reading ("seuen") to "twa" (Yorkshire 387).

283-86   Cf. <u>Apocalypse of Paul</u>: "And the angel came who was (appointed) over the punishments and he had a great blazing razor with which he lacerated the lips of that man and in the same way his tongue" (Hennecke 781).

304   When a pronoun accompanies the imperative form of the verb, the pronoun is generally in the nominative case (Mustanoja 475-76). In L, for both the singular and plural imperatives, the pronoun is, with two exceptions (504, 534), the reflexive accusative (Mustanoja 153). T always employs the reflexive accusative, while B consistently chooses the nominative.

308   In the right margin of B (fol. 12r.4) is the word "Slowth"; below are the words "Covetise" (fol. 12r.9) and "Lechory" (fol. 12r.14).

315   "þ[i]": The L scribe consistently uses the second-person possessive pronoun in this instance.

328   "bewar with me": 'take warning by me.' Instead of "with," B has "by," as does L at 465.

357   The fiery pits recall the <u>Apocalypse of Paul</u>: "And I saw to the north a place of varied and different punishments which was full of men and women, and a river of fire poured over them. And I looked and saw very deep pits and in them there were very many souls together..." (Hennecke 780).

369ff   Hanging is a commonplace in visions of torment. The <u>Apocalypse of Paul</u> supplies an early example: "And I looked and saw others hanging over a channel of water and their tongues were very dry.... And I saw other men and women suspended by their eyebrows and hair..." (Hennecke 783). In the <u>Legend of Saint Patrick's Purgatory</u> the sinful on the fourth plain are "hanging by burning chains from their feet, hands, hair, arms, or from their shins with their heads dangling in sulphurous flames. Others hang in fire, with iron hooks piercing their eyes, ears, noses, throats, breasts, or genitals" (D. D. R. Owen 42).

382ff   The earliest appearance of smiths in an afterlife vision is in the <u>Vision of Thespesius</u>: the demons at the three lakes, "like smiths, were using tongs to raise and lower alternately the souls of those whose wickedness was due to insatiable and overreaching avarice" (Plutarch 295). The <u>Voyage of Saint Brendan</u> contains a Laistrygonian-like episode on the island of smiths (D. D. R. Owen 23), while in the <u>Vision of Tundal</u> there is a description of the dungeon of smiths (lines 1030ff).

403   This peculiar spelling for the plural of <u>maiden</u>, unattested in the <u>MED</u> and <u>OED</u>, is allowed to stand, since it may well represent a feature of the Anglo-Irish dialect of the scribe, the doubling of final consonants, as in <u>bedde</u> (11), <u>didde</u> (425), etc. That it is an error, induced perhaps by "ankeresses" in the same line, is also arguable.

415   "prelates": 'persons of ecclesiastical authority, abbots, superiors of religious orders' [<u>OED Prelate</u>].

417   "lymys": 'territories, regions' [see <u>OED Limit</u>, <u>sb</u>. 3., where first illustrative quotation is 1494]. The phrase "in ȝour lymys and in ȝour suggetȝ" may well have the meaning ʹin your parishes and parishioners.'

430   "hert-strenges": 'region around the heart or tendons bracing the heart' [<u>MED</u> <u>herte</u> 1d.; see <u>OED Heart-strings</u> 1., where first illustrative quotation is ?1475/1483].

441   "degraded": 'debased <u>probably here with sense of</u> deprived of orders' [<u>MED</u> <u>degraden</u> (b)].

448   "þay": I.e., religious men and women.

449   The "strange whelys" which the devils "turned about with strange fyr...so fast þat...[the visionary] myȝt noȝt se ham" recall the fiery wheels in the <u>Apocalypse of Peter</u> (Hennecke 678). The "great, blazing wheel of iron" in the <u>Legend of Saint Patrick's Purgatory</u> is also turned "so swiftly...that it is impossible to see the sinners" (D. D. R. Owen 42). Os notes that the "burning wheel occurred in the classic vision (Aeneid, the wheel of Ixion) and...is likewise a feature of Islamic eschatology" (66). See Seymour 182 n.1, and Os 66 n.6, for other instances of the wheel in Christian visions.

454   "of religionse":   'of religious houses or
orders' [OED Religion 2.].   See the note at 44 on the
use of the similar substantive "religious."

484   "myshirynge":   'sinful hearing or listening'
[see OED Mishearing, where first illustrative quotation
is 1483].

505   "contenaunce":   '.conduct,   behavior'   [OED
Countenance I.1.].

519ff   A common method of cleaning rust from armor
and other metal gear was to roll it about in barrels
filled with sand and vinegar (Ffoulkes 79).

580   "þus myche":   'so much, as much as this' [OED
Thus, adv. 3.].

580-81   The ellipsis might be remedied by adding T's
"I   saw,"   but   elsewhere   L   is   elliptical   (590-91,
822-23).

591-93   "God hit þe ȝeld and al my helpers":   May
God reward you and all my helpers for it.'

599   "wel   of   mercy":   In   Saint   Bridget's
Revelations Christ refers to Mary as "a well moste
plenteous, oute of which mercy floweth vn-to wreches"
(54).   Chaucer uses the epithet in the Second Nun's
prologue, lines 36-37:   "Thow Mayde and Mooder, doghter
of thy Sone,/Thow welle of mercy, synful soules cure"
(Robinson 207).

611   "tribulaunce":   'tribulation, distress' [see
OED Tribulance, where first illustrative quotation is
1560].

627-30   The cat and dog appear at 74-75 and 193-94.
Cf. the Prioress in Chaucer's "General Prologue," lines
146-47,   and   see Robinson's bibliographical note for
"evidence that nuns were forbidden to keep dogs" (18,
654).

637   "my wikked angell":   "From the first century
onward it was, though not dogma, commonly believed
that, in addition [to a guardian angel], everyone had a
devil to tempt him.   That, at the hour of death, the
angel and the devil fought for the possession of the
soul was again merely a popular belief, the earliest

documentary evidence of which is to be found in the 7th century in the vision composed by St. Boniface" (Os 28).

664-76   On Margaret's transformation from black to red to white, see p. 12 above.

704   "reddur":   'torment, harsh treatment' [OED Reddour].

710   "euyn":   'settle or balance (an account), make compensation' [see OED Even, v. I.4., where first illustrative quotation is 1536]. The form of the verb is the subjunctive plural, governed by the phrase "many a man and womman þat."

712   "shrewed":   'bad, evil, or perhaps here having harmful consequences" [see OED Shrewd 3.b. and also 4., where first illustrative quotation is 1508].

723   "as":   T supports the emendation, as does L at 725.   See OED After IV.C.2.b. for the construction "after as."

723-24   The emendation from T corrects the homoeoteleuton in L.

748   "Euyn forth":   'straight on' [OED Even forth, adv. 1.].

749   For the plural noun "religions," see the notes at 44 and 454.

774-93   L's omission of the passage supplied by T is an instance of homoeoteleuton.   The L scribe apparently skipped from the word "purgatorye" in the phrase "The þrid purgatorye" to the same word in the final line, "And the third is the purgatory," necessitating the supralinear introduction of the verb "is."

775   "contenede":   'continued' [MED conteinen t.(a); OED contain II.17].   Horstman transcribes the word correctly but, apparently uncertain of the sense, suggests in a footnote "conceuede?" (Yorkshire 391).

794   In the right margin of L (fol. 164r.15) is the word "Nota."

822   "Southwich":   See the remarks on pp. 39-40 above.

830ff   See p. 18 above on the convention of weighing souls.

831   The white clothes of the "fayr lady" and "fayr yonge man" as well as the white cloth in which Margaret is wrapped (863-64) recall the imagery in Rev. 3.4-5 and 4.4. The Vision of Tundale likewise employs the imagery: "Hor clothis wer pracyows and new/As whytte as snow that euer dyd snew" (lines 1773-74).

833-35   In the heaven of the Vision of Tundale the builders of churches wear gold crowns and hold sceptres (lines 2061). Also see Rev. 4.4.

845-47   "þe quene of heuyn and of erth, emperice of helle and purgatory": In L late additions are the poems beginning "Myghtefful Mari y-crownyd quene/Emperesse off heuene and helle" (fol. 143v) and "Off mercy quene and emperesse" (fol. 145r).

859   "der": 'defy, challenge' [see OED dare B.II.5., where first illustrative quotation is 1580].

872   The reading "ouer" makes better sense than "on." The L scribe may have written "on," perhaps misreading an abbreviation (the u with a hook above it), or he may have written "ou," failing to make the abbreviation mark.

873   On the bridge into heaven or the earthly paradise, see p. 18 above.

881   "xiij men": The thirteen men are evidently representative of Christ and the twelve apostles.

882   See pp. 18-19 above on mystical weddings and ceremonies.

892   In the Apocalypse of Paul the entrance into paradise is likewise a golden gate: "And I followed the angel and he lifted me up to the third heaven and he set me at the door of a gate. And I looked at it and saw that it was a golden gate..." (Hennecke 771). In Saint Patrick's Purgatory the "prelates then led him [Owen] to the sloping side of a mountain, and bade him look up. He saw a place that seemed to be the colour of gold molten in the furnace. They told him that that was the gate of Heaven" (Seymour 174).

895-96   "þat Adam was in":   See the note at 173.
This reference to the earthly paradise is contra-
dictory, since Margaret has already enjoyed that
setting and is moving through the golden gate into
heaven.

TRANSLATION

A Note on the Translation

The aim of the translation is to make the medieval text accessible to students and scholars unfamiliar with Middle English but interested primarily in the text's contribution to women's studies and religious history. In the interests of clarity and readability, I take liberties with the original: I eliminate redundant words, such as simple connectives or the articles and prepositions repeated before elements in a series; I compress the expression "me tho3t" ('it seemed to me') to "it seemed" or "I felt"; if easily managed, I generally improve the agreement of subjects and verbs, pronouns and antecedents; I introduce subordinate conjunctions where a succession of coordinate conjunctions produces vagueness; and I frequently color repeatedly used adjectives, such as "strong" and "false," to enhance the sense. I leave Middle English words where no suitable translation is available (e.g., "worm," "adder," and "snake" are retained, though Middle English and modern meanings differ).

Those interested in an introduction to late Middle English popular prose will want to make the acquaintance of the critical text; with the support of this translation and the explanatory notes, a reader relatively unfamiliar with Middle English will find the fifteenth-century text manageable. The line numbers of the translation are made to correspond as closely as possible to the lines of the Middle English text, and asterisks signal relevant explanatory notes.

Translation of the Middle English Text

For everything begun that may bring profit   155r
to man's soul, may the credit be given to God
alone and to no earthly man or woman.   Dear
brothers and sisters, all who read this
narrative, listen and hear how a woman was
tormented in her sleep by a purgatorial spirit   5
and how she recounted her suffering to her
confessor.

My dear father, I wish to tell you of the
great tribulation I had in my sleep on the night
of St. Lawrence's Day,* the year of Our Lord
1422.   I went to bed at eight o'clock and fell   10
asleep.   And father, between nine and ten it
seemed I was seized and carried into purgatory,
where suddenly I saw all the pains that were
shown to me many times before--which you, father,
well understood from my recounting.*   But sir, on   15
this Saint Lawrence's night, I was not shown them
by any kind of spirit.*   But rather, father, it
seemed I saw them suddenly, and indeed, father,
never before had I been so terribly frightened
when I awoke from a vision of the pains as I was
then, and the reason was that I was not led by a   20
familiar spirit that might have comforted me.

And in this vision of purgatory, it seemed I
saw three great fires,* and it seemed that the
fires were end to end.   Moreover, sir, there was
no separation between them, but rather, each one   25
grew into the other.   And these three fires were
wonderful and horrible, and especially the
greatest of the three, for that fire was so

horrible and foul-smelling that all the creatures
in the world could not describe the wicked
stench. For in that fire were pitch and tar,   30
lead and brimstone, oil and everything that could
burn, and every kind of pain that man could
imagine, and every sort of Christian man and
woman living here in this world, no matter what
rank they were.   35
                                                         155v
     But among all the pains that I saw of all
men and women, it seemed priests who had been
lecherous in their lives, and their women with
them--whether they were religious or secular men
and women*--it seemed men and women in the   40
ministry of the Church had the greatest pain in
that sight. And in that great fire it seemed I
saw the spirit of a woman whom I had known
before, who had been in her life a sister in a
religious house and had been called Margaret. It   45
seemed I saw her in this horrible fire suffering
such great pains that I was too frightened to
describe them at that time.

     And in extreme terror I awoke. By that time
it was ten o'clock, and too anxious and fearful
to sleep again, I rose, and a little girl with   50
me,* and we two said the seven psalms and the
litany.* And by the time we had said the Agnus
dei, I was so sleepy I could not complete it, but
bade my child go to bed, and so did I. By then
it was eleven o'clock, and by the time I had   55
counted the last stroke, I fell asleep.

     And the spirit of this woman Margaret, whom
I had seen before in pains, came to me immediately, and it seemed she was marked with severe

wounds, as though she had been rent with combs.   60
And thus it seemed she was wounded and torn, but
especially, it seemed I saw at her heart a
grievous and horrible wound; from it there came
sparks, and from her mouth a flame.

And she said, "Cursed must you be and woe   65
befall you, unless you hasten to help me."

And it seemed that by the time she had
spoken these words, I was so frightened that I
could not speak, but constantly I thought, "The
Passion of Jesus be my help," and with that I was
spiritually comforted.   And then it seemed she   70
would have cast fire on me and rushed toward me
to kill me,* yet I felt she had no power, for the
Passion of God comforted me, though the grisly
sight of her frightened me.   And it seemed she
had a little dog and cat following her, all   156r
aflame.   76

And then it seemed I said to her, "What are
you, in God's name, who torment me so?   And I
conjure you in the name of the Father, the Son,
and the Holy Ghost, three persons in one God in   80
Trinity, that you tell me what you are who thus
torment me and whether you are a spirit from
purgatory seeking my help or a spirit from hell
seeking to overcome and trouble me."*

And she said, "No, I am not a spirit of hell   85
come to trouble you, but a spirit from purgatory
who wants your help.   And if you would like to
know what spirit I am that suffers great pains in
purgatory for my sin, I am the spirit of Margaret, who, as you know, was a sister living in a   90

religious house.   And in the name of God I ask
your help."

      And I asked her what I should do, and then
she said, "You must have thirteen masses said for
me in the manner I shall describe."   And then she   95
mentioned by name a good man, who was and is my
confessor.   "And ask him to say a mass of Requiem
for me.   And he must say for five days the entire
Miserere.*   And when he begins to say the
Miserere, may he say this verse, Miserere mei,   100
five times and then complete the psalm, casting
heart and eyes upward to God, for the more
devoutly he says it, the milder my pains will
surely be and the greater his reward.   And when
he has said this verse five times, let him   105
complete the psalm.   And ask him to say this hymn
Veni creator for five days.

      "Also, go to your priest, Sir John, and ask
him to say for me three masses of the Trinity and
the Miserere for five days with this hymn Veni   110
creator and so forth in the manner I described
before.

      "And also, send to your priest, the recluse
of Westminster, and ask him to sing three masses
of Saint Peter for me and for five days the
Miserere and the hymn Veni creator and so forth   115
in the prescribed manner.   And ask him to tell   156v
Don Peter Combe to say two masses of the Holy
Ghost for me and for three days the Miserere in
the manner described before and this hymn Veni
creator and so forth.   120

      "And ask Sir Richard Bone to say two masses
of Our Lady, Salue sancta parens, and for three

days the Miserere and the hymn Veni creator as
described above.

"And ask Don John Pery to say two masses of   125
All Saints, Gaudeamus, and three commemorations
of the Trinity and for three days the Miserere
and the hymn Veni creator as described above."

And then I asked her why she desired this,
to ask these masses to be said in this manner,   130
and she said there was no request that could help
her more quickly. And I asked why she desired
the Miserere to be said so often for her, and she
said in order to have the mercy and pity of
Almighty God, for as often, she said, as that
psalm, with this hymn Veni creator, is said for   135
her, as many pains would she be released from at
that time. And also, she said that if a man or
woman who is in fear of sin or in despair of
faith or God's mercy observes the practice of   140
saying this psalm with this hymn, he or she will
have true knowledge of this defect through the
power of God and will be delivered at that time
from that temptation through God's mercy. Also,
if a man or woman be tempted in any of the seven
deadly sins, as in theft, manslaughter,
slandering, backbiting, or any vile sin of   145
lechery, let him or her say with a good heart
these words Miserere mei deus, and the hymn Veni
creator in its entirety. The wicked spirits that
provoke him into that temptation will be expelled
instantly.   150

I asked of what profit it was to a soul to
say more masses of the Trinity, Our Lady, and
Saint Peter than it was of Requiem, and she said

that indeed there was nothing so profitable for a
soul--whoever might be able to do it--as to have   157r
said for it a hundred masses of the Trinity, a   156
hundred of Our Lady, fifty of Saint Peter, and a
hundred of Requiem,* and to say half a hundred
times after all these masses Miserere and Veni
creator. And for whatever sin he had done in his   160
life, no manner of purgatorial pain shall hold
him from which he will not be hastily delivered,
and many other souls will be delivered for his
sake. Moreover, if these masses are said for any
soul that is damned, yet shall the help and   165
benefit transfer to the next of kin and hastily
speed him out of his purgatory,* for that is a
place of mercy and cleansing for man's sin. And
nowhere else will they have so quickly such great
mercy that, through the power and mercy of God   170
and the virtue of these holy masses, they will
soon be delivered from their pains and led into
the earthly paradise, where Adam first lived,
there to be washed in the well of grace* with the
water of cleansing and to be anointed with the   175
oil of mercy.

   "For now I can tell you no more of the
bliss, for I know nothing yet but pains. And,
therefore, let whoever is able have these holy
masses said for him, and if he were in the
greatest pains of purgatory, he should soon be   180
delivered from them and from all others, if these
masses are said in the manner that I have
described to you, along with other good deeds and
almsgiving, according to the dead's wishes. And
if one is not able to have these masses said for   185

him, let him have these thirteen masses said for
him in the prescribed manner with <u>Miserere</u>
following and <u>Veni creator</u>. But the masses of
Our Lady shall be <u>Salue sancta parens</u>. And when
these masses are said, he or she will soon be   190
released from pain." And, father, all these
sights I had on the first night.

And then, father, when she had said all
these words, the little dog and cat that brought
her to me took her again to her pains. And yet,
before she went from me, she said I would surely
see her the next night in all her torments before   157v
she would come again to me. And she told how   196
seven devils would torment her, how the little
dog and cat would accompany her in the fire in
order to increase her pains, and how the worm of
conscience would continually gnaw her within.*
And the worm of conscience, she said, was the   200
greatest pain in purgatory or hell, for that, she
said, never ceased as long as one was in
purgatory.

And then I asked the spirit, "What do you
know of the pains of hell, since you have never
been there? How can you describe them any better   205
than you can the joys of heaven?"*

And then she said, "Indeed, by the
righteousness of God and by reason, I well know
that the worm of conscience is the most piercing
pain both here and there. But I cannot tell you   210
more about hell, for I have no permission, as
others have had who appeared to you before this.
And about heaven I told you before--how when I am
released from purgatory I will be lead into the

earthly paradise, washed and cleansed in the well   215
of grace, and anointed with the oil of mercy--and
I said I could not tell you more about heaven,
because I had not yet come therein. And
therefore," she said, "I tell you some
particulars concerning hell and some concerning
heaven." And with that word she said farewell   220
and spoke my name. "And tomorrow night take good
heed of my pains and also those of others, for
you will see both." And with that she went away
with a loud shriek and a great cry. And it seemed
she said, "O dear lady, help me." And then, my   225
dear father, soon afterwards I awoke, and by that
time it was one o'clock (I had fallen asleep as
it struck eleven).

And when I arose on the morrow, I went to   230
Master Forest, my confessor, and told him what he
should do for her, and indeed, he agreed
immediately.

I went to Sir John Wynbourne, my other
confessor, and told him what he should do for   235
her, and he agreed also, and so did all the
priests whom she had named to sing for her.

Now, father, on the very next night I went
to bed and fell asleep, and suddenly her
purgatorial pains and those of many others were   158r
shown to me. And, father, neither she nor any   241
other spirit led me, but rather, when I was
asleep, it seemed I saw them immediately without
a guide. And immediately it seemed I saw
Margaret in the worst clothes she had worn on
earth and in the greatest fire of the three,   245
which I had seen before in purgatory.

And it seemed I saw seven devils around her.
And one of them clothed her in a long gown with a
long train following her, and it was lined with
sharp hooks.   And it seemed the gown and the   250
hooks were all red fire.   And then that same
devil took worms, pitch, and tar and made curls
and set them upon her head, and he took a long,
large adder and wound it about her head, and it
seemed it hissed on her head as though it were   255
hot, burning iron in cold water.

And it seemed she cried when she was dressed
in this way so that all the world, it seemed,
might have heard her, and the little dog and cat
ripped to shreds her legs and arms.   260

And the devil that had dressed her so then
said, "This must you have for the foul, stinking
pride and ostentation that you practiced in the
world   instead   of   meekness.   And   for   your
excessive love for them on earth, this dog and   265
cat will constantly gnaw you while you are here.
For I am the devil of pride, and therefore, I
must do my duty in this pain and give you your
wages for the service that you have given me."
And it seemed many devils were with him.

And then it seemed six other devils quickly   270
came out, and one pulled out her tongue, and
another pulled out her heart, and it seemed they
raked it with iron rakes.   "And this," they said,
"you must suffer for your wrath and envy, for   275
oath-breaking, for backbiting and slandering--for
you practiced all of these in your life.   And we
are the devils of wrath and envy.   And all of
these adders and snakes that you see with us will

torment you for the wicked vices that you
practiced on earth, for which you failed to do   280
penance before you came here."

   And then it seemed two other devils came
out; one had sharp razors, and he acted as if he
would cut her flesh to pieces, and thus he did in
my sight.* And it seemed he pared away her lips,   158v
and he took a great hook of iron and thrust it   286
through her heart, and that other devil melted
lead and brimstone and every kind of stinking
poison that man could imagine. Also, he allotted
to her every kind of delicious food and drink,   290
which she had used in the world to provoke
herself more toward sin than virtue. And those
foods, it seemed, were all adders and snakes, and
they made her eat that against her will. And
they made her drink every kind of cursed poison   295
and said, "Eat and drink this for your stinking
gluttony and reckless spending, your wastefulness
and greed while you were alive." And then it
seemed these devils that cut away her flesh and
her lips and thrust the hook through her heart   300
drew her into deep, black water, and it seemed as
cold as ice, and much of it appeared to me to be
frozen. And in it they cast her and pushed her
up and down and said, "Take this bath for your
sloth and your gluttony." And then immediately   305
they took her out of the water and threw her into
a great fire, and there they made her remain.
And that, they said, should be her bed for the
sloth that she loved so well here on earth that
she would not come to God's service when she

might.   And there they made her remain, with many   310
worms about her.

And then it seemed two other devils came
out; one brought much gold and silver, and it was
melted and cast into her throat so that it ran
out of her stomach.   And he said, "Take this for   315
your cursed, wicked covetousness, for mismanaging
and misspending your money when you had it and
not helping others who had need."

And then it seemed that the other devil   320
brought her to a huge brass vat, and in it was
every kind of stinking thing and poison, and
worms both great and small.   And into this great
vat of very foul poison, they put her and pulled
her apart, limb from limb, and said, "Take this   325
bath for your vile, stinking lechery."

And, father, it seemed she cried horribly
and said, "Everybody take heed of me and do their
penance before they die and forsake the desire
for their wicked sins.   These two devils who   330
torment me here are the devils of covetousness
and lechery."

And so it seemed, my dear father, she was
tormented in these pains the length of half an   159r
hour.   And in all that time it seemed I did not   335
see her, but I heard her cry horribly, and many
times it seemed she said, "Dear Lady, help me."

And it seemed I stood alone and beheld her
pains and those of many a man and woman as well,
both secular and religous, wedded and single.   340
And it seemed I perceived, in the pains and
torments, whatever sin a man or woman had
practiced most while alive and which of the seven

sins each had loved best, everyone in his degree. But among all those pains and among all Christian people, it seemed lechery was the most severely chastised, and especially that of men and women of Holy Church, whether they were religious or secular. It seemed, father, that I saw priests and their women in pains, and for the most part they were bound together with iron chains. However, there were some priests who had women but were not bound to them as the others were, yet they had almost as much outward pain, it appeared, though not as much inward.

It seemed the pains of priests and their women were these. It seemed they were cast into dark pits full of intense fire,* and everything that might melt was thrown in with them to increase their pains. And it seemed the pit was full of adders, snakes, and wicked worms, and there it seemed the priests and their women were so tormented that all the creatures in the world would not know how to describe their pains. And it seemed, my dear father, they were taken out of the pit and cast into an extremely deep water, and it seemed that much of it was frozen, for it seemed as cold as ice. And there it seemed the devil completely drew apart their flesh with strong hooks.

And then, father, it also seemed that there hung over the water many high gibbets*--the sort men use to let a bucket down into a well to draw water from it--and these gibbets were equipped, it seemed, with sharp razors, and they were crooked, it seemed, as if they were hooks. And

345

350

355

360

365

370
159v

it seemed these razors were put in the priests'
throats and came out through their mouths. And
it seemed that the priests were plunged up and   375
down in that stinking water, the way men plunge a
bucket into a well, and when they were long
tormented, then they were taken down and brought
out of the water. And suddenly they were cast
into intense fires. And these devils cast oil
and grease on them and blew vigorously with   380
powerful bellows, so that I could see nothing of
them. And then soon after, it seemed these
devils laid them on anvils, as smiths do burning
iron, and struck them with hammers*--all those
priests, but not their women, for they were, it
seemed, freed from them. And then it seemed they   385
cried so horribly that all the world might not
make so horrible a noise and so hideous a cry.
And then it seemed that the devils took burning
metal, which seemed to be gold blended with
copper, and they put it, all hot, into the
priests' mouths, and it ran burning throughout   390
their bodies. And then a devil said, "Take this
sweet drink for deceitfully misspending God's
goods in cursed lechery, and in the practice of
your faithless gluttony and wicked pride."   395

Also, father, these devils took out the
priests' tongues, and it seemed they cut them in
two. And then it seemed these devils said, "Take
this pain in your tongues for the lying, foul,
slandering words of lechery that you spoke with   400
them and thereby brought many women to that sin
and out of their .good living--nuns, wives,
anchoresses, single women and maidens, and many

women who never would have done that sin. You,
with your sham gold and pleasing speech, have   405
prompted them to sin. They are here tortured
with you because of the lust and the covetousness
that they felt for you and your gold and because
they would not do penance before they died;   160r
therefore, they must pay dearly for it here."

    Then it seemed that the devils had many   410
sharp razors in their hands, and they pared off
the crowns--and it seemed the fingers and
lips--of some of those priests and said, "Take
this because you have misused them; and also
because you heads and prelates of Holy Church
should have chastised sin, both in yourselves and   415
your households, in your territories and your
subjects, and you did not; and because you
tolerated their covetousness of gold and their
flattering words, so that they might consent the
sooner to your will and do what you wished to   420
have done."

    And then it seemed the devils took burning
adders and put them into the priests' ears and
said, "Take this, for you were prelates of Holy
Church and would never hear the truth when you   425
did wrong, but utterly destroyed those who told
you anything against your will."

    And then it seemed the devils took out their
hearts, and in their hearts there was a fierce
worm, and it gnawed in two all their heartstrings   430
and internal organs. And then the devils said,
"Take this worm of conscience that will never
cease gnawing and chewing within until your sins
are forgiven. And it will do this because you

would not forsake your sin, nor do penance for   435
it, before you died. Also, very often you
received God very unworthily and handled him very
dishonorably, and that was because of your
stinking sin of lechery, as well as all other
sins against your conscience. Therefore, your   440
crowns and your fingers are pared away, and you
are degraded here for your abuse of your
priesthood."

And then it seemed I saw many devils run
about them and tear apart their privy members,
those of the priests and of their women as well.
But it seemed that religious men and women had a   445
hundred times more pain than secular priests and
secular women had, for they were cast onto cruel
wheels and turned about with intense fire,* and
adders, snakes, and devils were always around   450
them. And the devils turned the wheels so fast
that I could not see them, but very horribly they
cried, as if all the world had cried at once.
And this pain, father, had religious men and
women and prelates of Holy Church--more pain than   455
secular priests or secular women.

But all kinds of priests, and their women   160v
with them, were cast into deep pits. And very
horribly they cried together, and their cry was
this: "Woe befall pride, covetousness, and   460
lechery, and the wicked lusts of the world, and
woe befall the wicked-willed, who would never do
their penance here while they lived in this
wretched world. And therefore, here we shall pay
for it dearly, and may every Christian man and
woman take heed from us and forsake sin and do   465

penance in his life." And thus it seemed, my
dear father, I saw priests punished in purgatory.

And then, father, it seemed I suddenly saw
the pains of solitary nuns and monks and of all
other religious women, unaccompanied by a man, in   470
whatever state they stood in here. And father,
it seemed the pains of them were over intense,
burning fire. And the devils were ever raking on
them with strong hooks, the way, it seems, women
draw wool with combs. And they put every kind of   475
foul poison on them, and some took great, long
adders and serpents and thrust them burning
through their heads. And some put adders on
their heads, like garlands binding up their
foreheads, and it seemed each adder hissed upon
their heads as though it were burning iron in   480
cold water. And it seemed the devils took out
their hearts and pulled them apart with crooks.
And then the devils said to them, "Take here
these adders that run through your heads for your
sinful listening, for desiring more to hear vain
words to stir you to sin than to hear good words   485
that could stir you to the virtue that belongs to
your order. Also, take these adders that bind up
your foreheads for the seductive practice of
binding your foreheads when you were alive."   490

Also, father, it seemed the devils cut the
nuns lips in two, and the devils bade them take
that for lecherously kissing men and causing many
to fall into sin that otherwise would not have.   495
Also, it seemed that the devils cast upon their
heads veils of fire, which came down to their
brows. And then the devils said, "Take here

these veils for flagrantly showing your face in
your life--against your order--to stir yourselves   500
and others to sin."   161r

Then it seemed the devils took out their
tongues and set adders and toads on them, and
then the devils said, "Take this for your
deceitful lechery, foul words and foul behavior,
backbiting and slandering."   505

And then it seemed the devils came down and
completely tore apart their hearts and their
limbs. And then the devils said, "Take this for
your wicked sloth and fantasies, for your foul
behavior, and for the wicked thoughts that you   510
lay in."

And then it seemed they and the devils made
such a roaring that all the world, had they heard
it waking as I did sleeping, might have been
frightened by it. And this much, father, I saw   515
of the pains of religious men and women.

Then, father, soon after it seemed I saw the
pains of wedded men and women, and their pains
were these: they were put into great barrels
full of adders, snakes, and every other kind of   520
stinking thing. And it seemed the barrels were
firmly closed at both ends, so they were enclosed
within. And then it seemed the devils took long,
iron goads, all aflame, and put them through the
barrels, and as fast as they could, they turned   525
them about as men do to clean metal gear in
barrels of sand. And then it seemed the barrels
broke, and there burst out so much smoke that it
completely covered those who were about. And
then it seemed the devils took pitch and melted

it and put it into their throats; however, it did
not run through them but stayed within them. And   530
then it seemed the devils completely drew them
apart, bone from bone. And then the devils said
to them, "Take this bitter bath in these barrels
for your wicked, sinful lying in foul beds of   535
lechery and for faithlessly breaking your pledge,
against God's will, to keep yourselves to your
wives and to your husbands, as the law of God
would have you do. Also, take this bitter pitch
for the sweet foods and drinks that you, in your   540
gluttony, used to accomplish your lechery. Also,
take this bitter drawing apart for the soft beds
and soft clothing that you used to carry out your   161v
sin, and also for the wicked acts that you
performed against God's will and your
conscience." And thus it seemed I saw the pains   545
of wedded men and women.

And immediately after these, father, I saw
the pains of single men and women, and these it
seemed were that they were put on spits and
roasted, and as many adders, snakes, and toads,
along with as much foul poison as could swarm   550
about them, were set on them to suck and gnaw
them. And then they were taken off these spits,
both single men and women, and the devils drew
them throughout the fire with hard, sharp hooks.
And they completely pulled out their hearts and   555
their privy members. Then the devils said to
them, "Take these pains because you abused
yourselves in the foul lust of lechery and in all
other sins against God's will and your own
conscience, and because you abused yourselves in   560

the sin of lechery unnecessarily, since you might
have had and taken the freedom of wedlock, which
you had God's permission to take and which was
free and common to every man and woman not in
orders and under the law of God. And though you
might have done so and kept yourself from   565
lechery, you would not, but despised the order of
wedlock and feared that, if you were wedded,
other men would take your wives. And for this
foul mistrust and foul misuse of your body, take   570
here these bitter pains in purgatory and these
adders and snakes constantly gnawing on you until
your bonds of sin are wasted away and God has
shown you his mercy. For know well this is not
hell--this is an instrument of God's   575
righteousness to purge you of your sin in
purgatory. And take these pains because you
would not do penance in your lives before you
came here." And thus it seemed these devils said
to all these souls that were there. And this
much, my dear father, I saw of the pains of   580
single men and women, and all these it seemed I
saw from the time that the spirit of Margaret
left me.

And then she said to me, "Now you have seen
the bitter pains that I have suffered in these
great fires of purgatory." And then, father,   585
immediately it seemed that she came out of this
great vat and came to me. And then she said, "By
the devils who were my tormentors and by the
torments that they did to me, you can understand
what sins I have committed. And, therefore, now   590
they will never torment me further. May God   162r

repay you and all my helpers who have sped me out
of my pains."

And then I asked her why she had cried so
piteously, "Sweet Lady, help me," and why she had   595
cried more on Our Lady than on God Almighty or on
any other saint.   And then she said, "Indeed,
because she is the head of all other saints,
except God alone, and because she is the well of
mercy,* I cried to her in my great woe.   And
also, because I should be delivered the more   600
quickly through her request and prayer.   And
also, while I was alive, I kept her fast-day."
And the spirit said to me again that no one who
comes into purgatory who has fasted Our Lady's
fast before will fail to receive her help.   605

And then I asked her why she had cried so
dolefully in that great vat that she was in and
why I could not see her.   And then she said,
"Because my pains were so extreme, you would have
been so frightened if you had seen them that your
body would not well have borne your spirit   610
without great disturbance to your senses or else
severe sickness.   And therefore I cried so
horribly."

And then I asked her why that flame came out
of her mouth, why so many sparks came out of her   615
heart, why her heart was so wounded, why the
little dog and cat followed her, and what good
the masses and prayers did that she had asked to
have said for her.   And then she said, concerning
the flame from her mouth, that it was for the   620
great oaths that she had used in her life, and
further, concerning the wound at her heart (and

the sparks from it), that it was because her
oaths had been so troubling to Our Lord's heart
that the sparks of fire came out of her
heart--and that, she said, was one of the   625
greatest pains that she had. And, concerning the
little dog and cat, she said that they had been
her idols while she was alive and that she had
set her heart too much on such foul worms.*   630

    "And therefore, they shall always follow me
to increase my pains until the bonds of sin are
worn in two. And concerning the masses and the   162v
prayers said for me, they have hastened me more
quickly out of my pains. Also, henceforward I   635
will not be tormented further by devils, except
for one, who is my wicked angel, and he will
bring me through these two fires of purgatory.
And if there be any dross of sin, there will I be
cleansed, and this dog and cat will no longer   640
follow me."

    And then she said farewell and called my
name and said she would trouble me only one more
night in the vision of pains. And then it seemed
she went from me, but she did not cry as she had   645
before. And then, father, I awoke from my sleep,
and then it seemed I was very weary and
completely afraid. And father, this much I saw
on this night.

    And then, my dear father, it seemed she came
to me the following night. And father, it seemed   650
she was as black as lead, but she had no flame in
her mouth as she had had before, and also, the
wound at her heart was closed, and all the wounds
that it seemed she had had on her body before

were closed up. And then it seemed she said to
me, "Take good heed how I shall now be delivered   655
from my pains and move into the bliss of
paradise."

And then it seemed she left me. And
immediately a devil took her and threw her into
the middle fire. And there it seemed he had
bellows in his hand, and he blew hard, and it   660
seemed she lay and fried in the fire as though
she were a fish in hot oil. And then it seemed
he took her up again and led her throughout the
middle fire. And as she went, the blackness of
her body steadily fell away, like the tallow of a   665
candle when it drops from the heat. And by the
time that she came to the end of that great fire,
it seemed she had grown all red and well colored
like blood-red meat.

And then it seemed she entered into the   670
third fire, and this fire, it seemed, was as
clear as amber. And the devil brought her   163r
completely into it, and always as she went in
that fire, she grew ever clearer and clearer.
And it seemed she did not tarry in that fire, but
it seemed she hurried out of it, and by the time   675
she reached the end, she had grown wonderfully
white and fair.* And then it seemed she said,
"Blessed be God and Our Lady Mary that I am here
now. And God reward you and also those who have
helped me to arrive here so quickly. Had I not
had the grace of help, I would have been punished   680
in purgatory still three years longer. And had I
not appeared to you and received your help, I
would have had greater pain than I had."

And she said, "There are three purgatories.
One is the great fire of purgatory that you saw   685
me in first, and that is quite like the pains of
hell, except we shall be saved and they not. And
these other two fires are considered another."

And then I asked her if all who died would
go first to the great fire, and she said, "No,   690
Jews and Saracens die and other heathen people,
and they will never go there. They will go
straight to hell, because they will never be
saved. And all those who come into the great
fire of purgatory will be saved, no matter what
pains they are in."   695

And then I said to her, "I meant of all
Christian people--whether all Christian people
would go there before they went into the other
two fires."

And then she said, "No, sister, God forbid!
Many thousands go into the middle fire who do not   700
come into the great fire. And that is all those
who have contrition and have made satisfaction
and done penance for their sins. For," she said,
"the greatest fire is the harshest agent of the
justice of God in purgatory. Because," she said,   705
"all deadly sins men or women have committed in
this world, for which they have been shriven but
have not done penance before dying, will be
punished in this pain. Many men and women who
will not leave their sins or who make   163v
compensation suddenly before death takes them   711
will also be punished, along with many men and
women with many dangerous opinions. For they
will say that, if they may have three words

before death, they will not worry--and that is a
wicked, perilous statement!   But yet, God
mercifully grants to many these words when they   715
lie on their deathbeds, because it is very
displeasing to him to lose what he dearly bought.
And because of the diminishment of a man's senses
and the pains of his illness, he confesses and
absolves him as well as he can and puts him in
God's mercy. All these sorts of people will go   720
to this fire until the bonds of sin are wasted in
two, some longer and some shorter, and all
according to whether they have friends on earth
to help, have done good on earth before they
died, and have suffered sickness and tribulations   725
here. For," she said, "a day of sickness and
tribulation here will stand for a year in
purgatory, and that will be in the great fire.
But all who come into the greatest fire will come
through the middle fire and so likewise through
the clear fire and thus pass through the pains of   730
purgatory."

And she said, "Many will go through the
middle fire and not come into the great fire.
And those are they who have done many venial sins
and have been shriven of them only generally,
when some were to have been shriven of   735
particularly.   And many forgot sins or did
lenient or insufficient penance, or performed the
assigned penance too negligently with too little
repentance, or failed to fulfill before they died
penance that was enjoined: all these people will   740
be cleansed and will fulfill their penance in the

middle fire of purgatory and thus come out and
enter the third fire of cleansing, as I do now.

"And many go to the clear fire as soon as   745
they are dead and come neither into the great
fire, nor yet into the middle fire, but go right
to the clear fire and so straight on into bliss.
And they are innocents and holy religious men and
women, anchoresses, anchorites, and all holy   750
enclosed people, all holy martyrs and confessors,
and all kinds of Christian men and women in the
world, no matter what sin they committed, if
their penance was fulfilled before they died.
And through the mercy of God and the great trust   164r
in God or his mercy and through the contrition   755
that they have for their sin, as soon as they
die, they will come to this third fire of mercy
and so pass into the bliss of heaven without much
pain or hindrance."

And then, father, it seemed she said, "I   760
have shown to you these bitter pains of
purgatory, and I would show you two more
purgatories, but I may not stay longer. But this
is the general purgatory for all Christian men.

"And another is by sickness and great   765
tribulation in this world and through the
contrition they had and the pardon they purchased
for themselves in the world, while they were free
of deadly sin. For they may purchase themselves
so much pardon in this world that it will
counteract all the pains of purgatory and easily   770
bring them into the bliss of heaven. And this is
another purgatory: this is the purgatory of
mercy.

"The third is the purgatory of grace, and
that is, where one has most practiced and   775
continued his sins, there, if God will give him
grace, he will be punished and will not come into
the general pains of purgatory. And that is
called the purgatory of grace, but they will have
very great pains until God gives them mercy. And   780
many spirits appear to wakeful men on earth--and
in purgatory, too; they come to men and tell what
may help them, and thus they are delivered from
their pains. Also, many appear to men and women
while they sleep, as I did to you, and tell what   785
may help them and other friends. And all this is
the purgatory of grace, so I have recounted to
you three purgatories. One is the purgatory of
righteousness: that is, the general purgatory   790
that you have seen before. The other is the
purgatory of mercy. And the third is the
purgatory of grace, as I have told you.

"But let each man or woman who can, have
these masses said for him and the _Miserere_, with   795
this hymn _Veni creator spiritus_, in the manner I
have described before. And if one lacks the
power to have these masses said for him, let him
have these thirteen masses said for him with the
prayers following as previously described, and
God will through his mercy soon deliver him out   800
of his pain. And if there is any priest who will
say them for himself before he dies, they will
cancel his purgatorial pains when he comes
therein, as soon as they are said for him after
his death. Great grace and benefit he would   805
surely have from God for his effort. Or if he

would say these masses for any friend of his, it
would be better from him than from any other man,
and the more hastily will they be delivered out
of their pains for his good will and true labor." 810

And then she said, "Let every man and woman
who was hindered or in any temptation described
before say this hymn <u>Veni creator spiritus</u>, and
this temptation will soon disappear. And then
may he immediately thank God and receive his
mercy and say the <u>Miserere</u> and greet Our Lady
with five Aves."

164v
816

And then she said, "I have told you
everything as God desires and made an end of
purgatory. Take good heed of what you see me do 820
now. If you had not gone on pilgrimage for me to
Southwick in worship of God and Our Lady--for I
had vowed to do so and could not--I would be very
foully hindered in my passage when I am weighed 825
out of my pains, and that will you soon see."

And it seemed soon after there came a fair
lady and with her a fair young man, who seemed
about twenty years old. And he brought a pair of
scales in his hand, and he was clothed all in 830
white.* And it seemed the lady was clothed all
in white, with gold stars in her garment, a royal
gold crown on her head, and a sceptre in her
hand, on the end of which was a little cross.* 835
And then she spoke to the man in white: "Son,"
she said, "take this woman and let her be
weighed."

And then suddenly she was in the scales.
And immediately the devil and a great, long worm
were weighed against her, and twice she fell down 840

to the devil, who recounted all the sins for
which she had suffered. And then the man in
white said, "her sins are forgiven, because she
has done her penance for them, and she is given
to the well of mercy who is present here--the   845
queen of heaven and of earth, empress of hell
and purgatory, and the blessed mother of God.
This woman is given to her. What can you say to
this woman?"

     And then it seemed the devil took out a   850
great worm and said, "Here is the worm of
conscience that yet will trouble her for a thing   165r
that is behind: and that is, she made a vow to
make a pilgrimage and did not fulfill it."

     And then it seemed the fair lady said, "Here   855
is one who has done it for her, and my son and I
have given this woman mercy. And fie on you,
Satan! You and the worm of conscience will not
defy her further."

     And with that word it seemed she weighed   860
down to the fair lady. And it seemed the devil
and the worm made a great cry and immediately
vanished. And then the fair lady took a white
cloth and wrapped all about her and said, "Come
on with me, daughter, and you will receive the   865
oil of mercy, and your conscience will be made
clean. And all who helped you out of your pains
will have great reward. And when they must come
to purgatory, they will straightway find the
great mercy of Almighty God and the more quickly   870
be released from their pains for your sake."

     And then immediately the fair lady led her
over a strong bridge,* and at the end was a white

chapel.   And   it   seemed   a   great   multitude   of   875
people   came   out   in   a   beautiful   procession   and
with   a   merry   song.   And   then   this   fair   lady   and
the   procession   brought   her   to   a   well,   and   there
all   her   body   was   washed.   And   suddenly   beside   the
well   was   a   white   chapel,   and   this   lady   and   the
procession   brought   Margaret   therein.   And   880
immediately   thirteen   men   came   in,*   and   one   of
them   sang   a   mass.   And   it   seemed   the   fair   lady
offered   Margaret   to   him,*   and   suddenly   it   seemed
there   was   a   crown   placed   on   her   head   and   a
sceptre   in   her   hand.

    And   then   the   man   who   sang   the   mass   said,   885
"Daughter,   take   here   the   crown   of   grace   and   mercy
and   this   sceptre   of   victory,   for   you   are   past   all
your   enemies."   And   it   seemed   the   man   sang   out
the   mass,   and   when   the   mass   had   been   said,   165v
everyone   left   the   chapel.   And   the   man   who   sang   890
the   mass   took   Margaret   with   him   and   brought   her
to   a   golden   gate*--and   the   procession   with
them--and   he   said   to   Margaret,   "Daughter,   go   in
at   this   gate   and   receive   the   bliss   of   paradise
and   heaven,   your   natural   inheritance,   where   Adam   895
once   lived."

    And   then   I   awoke   and   everything   had
vanished.   No   more,   father,   at   this   time.   But
may   God   bring   us   to   his   kingdom.   Amen.

WORKS CONSULTED

Allen, Hope Emily. Writings Ascribed to Richard Rolle, Hermit of Hampole, and Materials for His Biography. London: Oxford UP, 1927.

Apocalypse: The Morphology of a Genre. Ed. John J. Collins. Semeia 14 (1979).

Atkinson, Clarissa W. Mystic and Pilgrim: The Book and the World of Margery Kempe. Ithaca: Cornell UP, 1984.

Attwater, The Penguin Dictionary of Saints. 2nd ed. Rev. by Catherine Rachel John. 1965. New York: Penguin, 1983.

Bede. Historia ecclesiastica. Ed. Bertram Colgrave and R. A. B. Mynors. Oxford: Oxford UP, 1969.

Benskin, Michael. Letter. 20 June 1985.

----------. Letter. 12 October 1982.

Benskin, Michael, and Angus McIntosh. "A Mediaeval English Manuscript of Irish Provenance." Medium Aevum 41 (1972): 128-31.

Bernstein, Alan E. "Esoteric Theology: William Auvergne on the Fires of Hell and Purgatory." Speculum 57 (1982): 518-19, 523.

Bloomfield, Morton W. The Seven Deadly Sins: An Introduction to the History of a Religious Concept, with Special Reference to Medieval English Literature. N.p.: Michigan State College P, 1952.

Bogin, Meg. The Women Troubadours. New York: Norton, 1976.

The Book of Margery Kempe. Ed. Sanford Brown Meech. Prefatory note by Hope Emily Allen. EETS os 212. London: Oxford UP, 1940.

Brewer, D. S., and A. E. B. Owen, introd. The Thornton
    Manuscript (Lincoln Cathedral MS. 91). London:
    Scolar P, 1975.

Butler's Lives of the Saints. Ed., rev., and suppl. by
    Herbert Thurston and Donald Attwater. 4 vols.
    London: Burns and Oates, 1956.

Calendar of Entries in the Papal Registers Relating to
    Great Britain and Ireland: Papal Letters, 1198-
    1404. Eds. W. H. Bliss and J. A. Twemlow. 6
    vols. London: Mackie, 1904.

Calendar of the Patent Rolls Preserved in the Public
    Record Office: Henry IV, 1422-29. Norwich:
    Norfolk Chronicle, 1901.

Cevetello, J. F. X., and R. J. Bastian. "Purgatory."
    The New Catholic Encyclopedia. 1967 ed.

Clay, Rotha Mary. The Hermits and Anchorites of
    England. 1914. Detroit: Singing Tree P, 1968.

Collis, Louise. Memoirs of a Medieval Woman: The Life
    and Times of Margery Kempe. 1964. New York:
    Harper, 1983.

The Compotus Rolls of the Obedientiaries of St. Swi-
    thun's Priory, Winchester. Ed. G. W. Kitchin.
    London, 1892.

Cooper, Thompson. "Ives, John." DNB (1896).

----------. "Martin, Thomas." DNB (1896).

Dante. Purgatory. Trans. Dorothy Sayers. 1955. New
    York: Penguin, 1969.

Deanesly, Margaret, ed. The Incendium Amoris of
    Richard Rolle of Hampole. London: Longmans,
    Green, 1915.

Dearmer, Percy. The Legend of Hell: An Examination of
    the Idea of Everlasting Punishment, with a Chapter
    on Apocalyptic. London: Cassell, 1929.

De Guileville, Guillaume. The Booke of the Pylgremage
    of the Sowle. Ed. Katherine Isabella Cust.
    London, 1859.

Deguileville, Guillaume de. The Pylgremage of the
    Sowle. The English Experience: Its Record in
    Early Printed Books Published in Facsimile 726.
    Norwood, N.J.: Johnson, 1975.

The Dialogues of Saint Gregory, Surnamed the Great.
    Trans. and ed. Edmund G. Gardner. London:
    Warner, 1911.

Doyle, A. I. Letter. 27 October 1980.

Dronke, Peter. Women Writers of the Middle Ages: A
    Critical Study of Texts from Perpetua to Mar-
    guerite Porete. Cambridge, Eng.: Cambridge UP,
    1984.

Emden, A. B. A Biographical Register of the University
    of Oxford to A. D. 1500. London, 1957.

Ffoulkes, Charles. The Armourer and His Craft from the
    XIth to the XVIth Century. 1912. New York:
    Noble, 1967.

Fletcher, William Younger. English Book Collectors.
    London: Paul, Trench, Trubner, 1902.

Flete, John. The History of Westminster Abbey. Ed. J.
    A. Robinson. Cambridge, Eng.: Cambridge UP,
    1909.

Foster, Frances A. "Legends of the After-Life." In A
    Manual of the Writings in Middle English:
    1050-1500. Gen. eds. J. Burke Severs and Albert
    E. Hartung. 6 vols to date. Hamden, Conn.:
    Conn. Academy of Arts and Sciences, 1967- .
    2:452-57, 645-49.

Gies, Frances, and Joseph Gies. Women in the Middle
    Ages. New York: Crowell, 1978.

Greg, W. W. The Calculus of Variants: An Essay on
    Textual Criticism. Oxford: Clarendon, 1927.

Halliwell, J. O. The Thornton Romances. London, 1844.

Hanna, Edward J. "Purgatory." The Catholic Encyclo-
    pedia. 1913 ed.

Harley, Marta Powell. "A Revelation of Purgatory: A
    Critical Edition Based on Longleat MS. 29." Diss.
    Columbia U, 1981.

Hazlitt, W. Carew. A Roll of Honour: A Calendar of
    the Names of Over 17,000 Men and Women Who
    throughout the British Isles and in Our Early
    Colonies Have Collected MSS. and Printed Books
    from the XIVth to the XIXth Century. London,
    1908.

Hennecke, E. New Testament Apocrypha. Ed. W. Schnee-
    melcher. Trans. R. McL. Wilson. 2 vols. London:
    Lutterworth P, 1965. Vol. 2.

Himmelfarb, Martha. Tours of Hell: An Apocalyptic
    Form in Jewish and Christian Literature.
    Philadelphia: U of Pennsylvania P, 1983.

Hirsch, J. C. "Author and Scribe in The Book of
    Margery Kempe." Medium Aevum 44 (1975): 145-50.

Hodgson, Geraldine E., trans. The Form of Perfect
    Living and Other Prose Treatises by Richard Rolle
    of Hampole. London: Baker, 1910.

Hollenbach, M. W. "Synderesis." The New Catholic
    Encyclopedia. 1967 ed.

The Holy Bible: Douay Version. London, 1956.

Horrall, Sarah M. "The Watermarks on the Thornton
    Manuscripts." Notes and Queries ns 27 (1980):
    385-86.

Jacobus de Voragine. The Golden Legend. Trans.
    Granger Ryan and Helmut Ripperger. 2 vols.
    London: Longmans, Green, 1941.

Julian of Norwich. A Revelation of Love. Ed. Marion
    Glasscoe. Exeter: U of Exeter, 1976.

----------. Revelations of Divine Love. Trans.
    Clifton Wolters. 1966. New York: Penguin, 1984.

Kane, George, ed. Piers Plowman: The A Version. Will's Visions of Piers Plowman and Do-Well. London: Athlone P, 1960.

Keiser, George R. "Lincoln Cathedral Library MS. 91: Life and Milieu of the Scribe." Studies in Bibliography 32 (1979): 158-79.

----------. "A Note on the Descent of the Thornton Manuscript." Transactions of the Cambridge Bibliographical Society 6 (1976): 346-48.

Knowles, David. The Religious Orders in England, Volume 2: The End of the Middle Ages. Cambridge, Eng.: Cambridge UP, 1955.

Knowles, David, and R. Neville Hadcock. Medieval Religious Houses: England and Wales. 1953; London: Longmans, Green, 1971.

Krapp, George Philip. The Legend of Saint Patrick's Purgatory: Its Later Literary History. Baltimore: Murphy, 1900.

Leland, John. The Itinerary of John Leland in or about the Years 1535-43. Ed. Lucy Toulmin Smith. 5 vols. 1907. Carbondale: Southern Illinois UP, 1964. Vol. 1.

The Life of Saint Katherine. Ed. E. Einenkel. EETS os 80. London, 1884.

Louvet, M. L'abbé. Le Purgatoire d'après les révélations des saints. 3rd ed. Paris, 1893.

Manly, John M., and Edith Rickert. The Text of the Canterbury Tales. 8 vols. Chicago: U of Chicago P, 1940. Vol. 1.

McGinn, Bernard. Visions of the End: Apocalyptic Traditions in the Middle Ages. N.Y.: Columbia UP, 1979.

McIntosh, Angus. Letter. 26 May 1985.

----------. "A New Approach to Middle English Dialectology." English Studies 44 (1963): 1-11.

McIntsoh, Angus, and M. L. Samuels. "Prolegomena to a Study of Mediaeval Anglo-Irish." Medium Aevum 37 (1968): 1-11.

McMillan, Ann. "'Fayre Sisters Al': The Flower and the Leaf and The Assembly of Ladies." Tulsa Studies in Women's Literature 1 (1982): 27-42.

Medieval Libraries of Great Britain. Ed. N. R. Ker. 2nd ed. London: Royal Historical Society, 1964.

Michel, A. "Feu du Purgatoire." Dictionnaire de Théologie Catholique. 1936 ed.

----------. "Purgatoire." Dictionnaire de Théologie Catholique. 1936 ed.

The Mirrour of the Blessed Lyf of Jesu Christ. Ed. Lawrence F. Powell. Oxford: Oxford UP, 1908.

Moore, Samuel, S. B. Meech, and Harold Whitehall. "Middle English Dialect Charcteristics and Dialect Boundaries." Essays and Studies in English and Comparative Literature 13 (1935): 1-60.

Mosse, Fernand. A Handbook of Middle English. Trans. James Walker. Baltimore: Johns Hopkins P, 1952.

Mustanoja, Tauno F. A Middle English Syntax. Mémoires de la Société Néophilologique de Helsinki 23. Helsinki: Société Néophilologique, 1960.

Nixon, Howard M. Letter. 2 August 1982.

Norriss, Rev. V. W. Letter. 16 July 1982.

"Notable Accessions." The Bodleian Library Record 2 (1941-49): 169-70.

Oakden, J. P. Alliterative Poetry in Middle English: The Dialectal and Metrical Survey. Manchester: Manchester UP, 1930.

Ogden, Margaret S., ed. The Liber de Diversis Medicinis in the Thornton Manuscript. EETS os 207. 1938. London: Oxford UP, 1969.

Ogilvie-Thomson, Sarah Jane. "An Edition of the English Works in MS. Longleat 29 excluding The Parson's Tale.'" Diss. Oxford U, 1980.

Os, Arnold B. van. Religious Visions: The Development of the Eschatological Elements in Mediaeval English Religious Literature. Amsterdam: Paris, 1932.

Owen, A. E. B. "The Collation and Descent of the Thornton Manuscript." Transactions of the Cambridge Bibliographical Society 6 (1975): 218-25.

Owen, D. D. R. The Vision of Hell: Infernal Journeys in Medieval French Literature. Edinburgh: Scottish Academic P, 1970.

Patch, Howard Rollin. The Other World According to Descriptions in Medieval Literature. Smith College Studies in Modern Languages ns 1. Cambridge, Mass.: Harvard UP, 1950.

Pearce, E. H. The Monks of Westminster. Cambridge, Eng.: Cambridge UP, 1916.

Pearsall, Derek A., ed. The Floure and the Leafe and The Assembly of Ladies. London: Thomas Nelson, 1962.

Petti, Anthony G. English Literary Hands from Chaucer to Dryden. Cambridge, Mass.: Harvard UP, 1977.

Plutarch. "On the Delays of the Divine Vengeance." In Moralia. Trans. Phillip H. de Lacy and Benedict Einarson. 15 vols. Cambridge, Mass.: Harvard UP, 1968. 7:170-299.

Power, Eileen. Medieval English Nunneries. 1922. New York: Biblo and Tannen, 1964.

The Register of the Common Seal of the Priory of St. Swithun, Winchester, 1345-1497. Ed. Joan Greatrex. Hampshire Record Series 2. N.p.: Hampshire County Council, 1978.

The Revelations of Saint Birgitta. Ed. William P. Cumming. EETS os 178. London: Oxford UP, 1929.

Ricci, Seymour de. English Collectors of Books and Manuscripts, 1530-1930, and Their Marks of Owner-ship. Cambridge, Eng.: Cambridge UP, 1930.

Robinson, F. N., ed. The Works of Geoffrey Chaucer. 2nd ed. Boston: Houghton Mifflin, 1957.

Rolle, Richard. The Fire of Love. Trans. Clifton Wolters. 1972. New York: Penguin, 1981.

Rye, Walter. "Le Neve, Peter." DNB (1896).

Seymour, John D. Irish Visions of the Other-World: A Contribution to the Study of Mediaeval Visions. New York: MacMillan, 1930.

Shahar, Shulamith. The Fourth Estate: A History of Women in the Middle Ages. Trans. Chaya Galai. New York: Methuen, 1983.

Sotheby and Company. Catalogue of Fine Illuminated Manuscripts, Valuable Printed Books, Autograph Letters, and Historical Documents. London: n.p., 1946.

Southern, R. W. "Between Heaven and Hell." Rev. of La Naissance du Purgatoire, by Jacques le Goff. Times Literary Supplement 12 June 1982: 651-52.

Spencer, Theodore. "Chaucer's Hell: A Study in Mediaeval Convention." Speculum 2 (1927): 177200.

Stanley, Arthur P. Historical Memorials of Westminster Abbey. 3rd and rev. ed. London, 1869.

Stone, Robert Karl. Middle English Prose Style: Margery Kempe and Julian of Norwich. The Hague: Mouton, 1970.

Thompson, E. M., et al. The New Palaeographical Society: Facsimiles of Ancient Manuscripts. Second Series (1913-14).

The Three Kings of Cologne. Ed. C. Horstman. EETS os 85. 1886. New York: Kraus, 1973.

Utley, Francis Lee. "Dialogues, Debates, and Catechisms." In A Manual of the Writings in Middle English: 1050-1500. Gen. eds. J. Burke

Severs and Albert E. Hartung. 6 vols. to date. Hamden, Conn.: Conn. Academy of Arts and Science, 1967- . 3:698-700, 864-65.

The Victoria History of Hampshire and the Isle of Wight Ed. H. Arthur Doubleday and William Page. 5 vols. Westminster: Whitehall, 1900-03; London: Constable, 1908-12.

The Visions of Tundale, Together with Metrical Moralizations and Other Fragments of Early Poetry. Ed. W. B. D. D. Turnbull. Edinburgh, 1843.

Visitations of Religious Houses, Volume 1: 1420-1436. Ed. A. Hamilton Thompson. Horncastle, Eng.: Morton, 1914.

Walcott, Mackenzie E. C. Memorials of Christchurch-Twynham. 3rd ed. Rev. by B. Edmund Ferrey. Christchurch, 1883.

Wykeham's Register. Ed. Thomas Frederick Kirby. 2 vols. London, 1896.

Yorkshire Writers: Richard Rolle of Hampole, an English Father of the Church, and His Followers. Ed. C. Horstman. 2 vols. New York, 1895.

STUDIES IN WOMEN AND RELIGION

DATE DUE

HIGHSMITH   #LO-45220